CROSSROADS

RANDOM HOUSE

NEW YORK

CROSSROADS

The Future of American Politics

ANDREW CUOMO

Editor

Copyright information for the essays contained in this volume can be found on page 299.

RANDOM HOUSE and colophon are registered trademarks of Random House, Inc.

LIBRARY OF CONGRESS CATALOGING-IN-PUBLICATION DATA

Crossroads: the future of American politics / [edited by] Andrew Cuomo.
p.   cm.
ISBN 1-4000-6145-8
1. Democratic Party (U.S.)   2. United States—Politics and government—2001–
I. Cuomo, Andrew Mark.

JK2316C76 2003
324.2736—dc21   2003054764

Design by Meryl Sussman Levavi

Printed in the United States of America on acid-free paper

Random House website address: www.atrandom.com

9   8   7   6   5   4   3   2   1

First Edition

To my daughters, Cara, Mariah, and Michaela,
and the hope that we leave you the world stronger
and sweeter than we found it

Contents

CONTENTS

Introduction

Andrew Cuomo

THE AGONY OF DEFEAT. IT SEEMS MAGNIFIED IN A POLITICAL ELEC-
tion, that modern-day crusade and zero-sum game. There is no silver medal awarded for finishing second. Elections consume body
and soul.

My race was great political theater. I was running last year
in a primary to challenge George Pataki, who defeated my father,
Mario Cuomo. The New York press had choreographed the campaign into an Italian opera in which the son was to avenge the father's death. Unfortunately the conclusion did not support the
premise. There is no romance in the opera: father dies, and then
son dies.

Political loss is unique in that it is public and pervasive. There is no need to whisper in the kitchen, "Honey, I didn't get the promotion." After an unsuccessful political campaign, everyone knows you lost.

For me, the pervasive nature of loss became real one day after my withdrawal from the New York governor's race, when I was at a gas station. I pulled into the self-service island and removed the gas cap. I was exercising all deliberate caution not to dirty my suit or my tie, which had a proclivity to position itself as a bib for the gas nozzle. I was attempting my personal innovation: wedging the gas cap into the nozzle to avoid having to hold the handle. As this is not easily done, I made several attempts in which the cap fell down and rolled to some inaccessible spot, causing me to have to retrieve it, moving delicately to avoid dirtying myself. I eventually gave up and became resigned to holding the handle myself. At this point I looked across the island to see the customer on the other side watching my exhibition. The patron across the way looked at me and said, "Boy, Andrew, losing really stinks—you even have to pump your own gas."

Everyone knew. There was no hiding.

A political campaign is not only extraordinarily public, but also personally taxing. It puts tremendous strain and pressure on the candidate and those closest to the candidate. Friends are called on for help—again and again. Family relations are stressed by combining professional responsibilities and personal issues: sometimes to the breaking point. Loss often compounds the cost. But, however painful, political candidates and their parties must withstand bitter defeats in order to learn, grow, and improve. In a very real way—sometimes too real for those of us who have run and lost—American democracy teaches humility not only for its own sake but also for the ultimate public interest. For as Hubert Humphrey said, "There is a lot of difference between failure and defeat. Failure is when you are defeated and neither learn nor contribute anything." If we learn from our defeats, grow from the experience, and listen once again and more closely to the voices of the people, then we may better serve our country and our communities.

I chose to compile this book after my own defeat. It has been a time of personal and professional reflection. Its rationale is twofold: first, for many reasons, our governments at every level are being called upon to play increasingly profound roles in our lives, to protect not only our physical security but also our values, in unprecedented ways. Politics is our vehicle to produce leaders who not only reflect our values but also apply them creatively; and second, I still believe in what I campaigned on even though I didn't win. This is a time of great new challenges, and we need new ideas and new approaches.

America is at a crossroads. We live in a time of fundamental power shifts and power vacuums, where America is the lone superpower for the first time, and is both the tamer and target of an unstable world. We live in a new information age where the wealth of a country depends more on the fertility of its minds than the fertility of its soil. Our population is slowly but inexorably aging, and the coming octogenarian boom will put the greatest burden on government services in the history of our nation. We are now saddled with the largest federal budget deficit on record. There are indications that our consumption and dependence on fossil fuels are causing permanent changes in our climate—perhaps minor and insignificant, perhaps major and devastating. And many of our most stubborn problems remain—race relations, poverty, failing public education, housing shortages, and the widening gulf between the wealthy and everyone else.

On top of the domestic challenges, while the international scene continues to shift on a daily basis, unquestionably there will be new security threats and new diplomatic issues for this country to deal with in the months and years ahead.

Finally, one trend that is truly frightening to me is the alienation of young people from both our political parties. Young people volunteer less, vote less, and participate less in the political process.

Voting rates among those voters under the age of twenty-five declined from 40 percent in 1980 to just 26.3 percent in 2000.

I believe in checks and balances and the two-party system. Each party serves the nation better when faced with stiff opposition from the other party. The old adage is true: your game is only as good as the person on the other side of the net. To that end, a vigorous debate between two viable parties (at a minimum) is essential.

This book seeks to frame and inform that debate: Do the Democrats "get it" and are they poised for a comeback? Has the Republican Party successfully repositioned itself as the majority party? Can young people become a vital political force? Have both parties lost sight of the central principles that attract voters, and do they focus less on finding real solutions to the challenges Americans face and more on finding the quick political message that will produce victory?

I have asked forty-one of the nation's most thoughtful citizens to address the current state of American politics, using the 2002 elections as a reference point. They represent a diverse range of opinion and expertise.

The essays herein defy easy summary or sound bite. However, certain common themes emerge.

In personal and broad-ranging essays, the current Democratic candidates for president—Dean, Edwards, Gephardt, Kerry, Lieberman, Graham, Moseley Braun, and Sharpton—each stress different areas of policy, but all assert that the Democratic Party, and its leaders, must be a party greater than the sum of its policy positions. And each writer goes to different fountains for inspiration: faith, family, sacrifice, justice, and fiscal stewardship are central among these.

Leaders of both parties, and the strategists who advise them, remind us that it is not enough to stay "on message"; you also need a message that truly reflects hard thinking about the problems people face and that offers solutions that transcend party labels. Whether Democrat or Republican, the political leaders gathered in this volume almost universally express a deep concern about the fact that both major parties often care more about winning than about the task of governing with clear principles and sound solutions. They warn that in the age of the twenty-four-hour media cycle, the focus of politics too often shifts away from addressing common problems and real solutions to leveraging short-term political advantage for electoral gain. And they caution that getting elected and governing are two entirely different challenges.

Lest we lose historical perspective, Joseph Ellis, Norman Ornstein, and others remind us that many of the predictions of lasting Republican hegemony are about as likely to come true as any Nostradamus prediction. In particular, the hubris bred by success at the polls and the checks and balances inherent in our government (thanks to the Founders, we are wisely reminded) will provide Democrats an opening sooner or later. Echoing a theme of this volume, Ellis also predicts that, in an era of daunting challenges just over the horizon, "true American statesmanship will come to depend on the simple talent for straight talk."

Peggy Noonan chooses a blunter tool to make a similar critique of the Democratic Party: Democrats have become "snobs" who are out of touch with common concerns and foolishly remain loyal even to those without a real plan for the future. Fellow Republican Peter Peterson suggests that both parties have lost sight of the common good, whether in blind pursuit of tax cuts and deficit spending (Republicans) or through the untamed growth of entitlements (Democrats). In the same vein, Al From and Bruce Reed urge Democrats to expand our appeal beyond the party's traditional base and seek policy solutions from outside the usual Democratic toolbox. Bernard Goldberg and Richard Cohen hark back to a time when the Democratic Party possessed such broader appeal as a matter of course, and explore the reasons why we have, in their view, lost that appeal. In an in-depth analysis of Senator Mary Landrieu's victory—a lone bright spot for Democrats in 2002—Professor Douglas Brinkley brings former Speaker Tip O'Neill to mind when he says that amid all our discussion about party principles and national trends, we cannot forget that all politics is local: the Bush administration's policies favoring importation of sugar from Mexico, for example, can make the difference in a tight race. Kate Michelman, a tireless advocate to protect reproductive rights, says that women are the key to electoral success for Democrats and are still an untapped reservoir of ideas for rejuvenating the party.

The 2002 elections, like all elections, involved important demographic preferences that neither party can ignore. John DiIulio, Jr. and Georgette Mosbacher raise a red flag for Democrats who have collectively alienated many religious voters and failed to energize minority voters or attract aging baby boomers. Sean Wilentz blames Republican officials for suppressing the African-American vote in key areas. Russell Simmons makes clear in his essay, as he has done in his establishment of the Hip-hop Summit Action Network, that we cannot overcome poverty or ignorance without educating, energizing, and organizing young people in this nation. Harvard students Andrew Frank, Ganesh Sitaraman, and Joel Washington sound this alarm as well (though from opposite ends of the ideological spectrum) and propose specific steps to inspire our youth to political action.

Together, these essays form a mosaic of politics in America during one of the seminal moments in our country's history. Each writer in his or her own way voices concern about governance and a political system that can and must do better. And each offers insights into how to improve our government and make the right choices at these crossroads to keep America strong, prosperous, principled, just, and free.

Read the essays for what they say and what is left unsaid. To identify a void is also instructive.

As the saying goes, in these times it seems the only constant is change. As we navigate our way through these troubled and changing times these opinions can offer insights. Politics at its best is an exchange of ideas: an honest debate on the problems and solutions of the time.

Let the debate begin!

CROSSROADS

Letter from a Democratic Party Pooper

Tim Ashe

A master's student at Harvard University's Kennedy School of Government, TIM ASHE formerly worked on the staff of Congressman Bernie Sanders in Vermont, where he resides.

THE EMPEROR CAN CHANGE HIS CLOTHES, BUT HE'LL STILL BE naked. This extension of the classic fable lies at the heart of the failure of national Democrats to capture the imagination (and needed votes) of the electorate. It also explains why I left the Democratic Party.

Two story lines in the Democrats' operatic departure from a cogent belief set explain why Republicans have made such major gains in recent years at the federal, state, and local levels. First, the Democratic Leadership Council has successfully, though never substantively, argued that the American voter is in the middle. Second, while the Republicans put up a united front with a lockstep set of positions on key issues, the Democrats have been drifting, aimlessly "appealing" to one voter bloc or another. This second point not only suggests the need for a reaffirmation of core party beliefs, but also questions whether the current party leadership will be able to turn this tragic play into a comedy.

In July 2001, a freelance writer confronted President Bush in a greeting line and told him he was disappointed with his performance to that point. Bush, responding with customary charm, allegedly said, "Who cares what you think?" Before turning to a discussion of the recent failings of the Democratic Party, let me tell you why you should care what I think.

I should be a Democrat. From Massachusetts, mother a teacher and father a civil servant, family of Kennedy-philes, student at the Kennedy School of Government. Most important, onetime Democratic voter. I've got a long life of political activism ahead of me. My loyalties are to ideas and not a party, so if my energies are not going to the Dems, they'll be going somewhere else. It's up to the leadership of the party to decide whether people like me will return to and someday lead the party that once stood more strongly and clearly for the average citizen.

So Who Is a Liberal?

Al From, Bruce Reed, and others who subscribe to the moderating tendencies of the Democratic Leadership Council would have us believe that the majority of Americans are center or just right of center on the political spectrum. As evidence, they cite various polls in which registered voters more often than not self-identify as somewhat or mostly conservative. Anything, that is, except a liberal. And so, the logic goes, the Democratic Party needs to move to the center because that's where the voters are.

There are two critical points that call these self-identifying polls into question. First, the very word *liberal* has followed the path of "political correctness." In other words, it's pejorative. It's a badge of shame that emasculates men and radicalizes women. And in a cruel marriage that has Tom DeLay licking his lips, it's not uncommon to hear today's iconoclastic media figures referring to one or another "politically correct liberal." The labels make matters exponentially worse when coupled: "tax-and-spend liberals," or, better yet, "Kennedy liberals." Any observer with an ear to the ground can agree that most people (including many members of Congress) want to be called a liberal like they want to drink poison.

Can we trust the instinct to move to the center? Can Democrats afford to lurch yet farther to the middle because a sample of voters will not say that they are liberal? Perhaps an appropriate manner of answering these questions, and to get to the second point, is to put the onus on the moderating forces of the party to explain what is, to understate slightly, an enormous problem with their logic.

Polls show that a majority of Americans do not want to label themselves "liberal." Fair enough. But polls *also* show that most Americans, in fact large majorities, strongly support so-called liberal positions on health care, Social Security, and education. Same goes for the environment, a living wage, and programs for people with disabilities. What do we make of this voter, who calls himself "somewhat conservative" while standing ideologically with the liberal wing of the Democratic Party on almost every issue of substance? A conservative? That doesn't seem to fit quite right. A liberal? Well, not by the voter's own admission. To take an example from my adopted home state, how do we explain the fact that a majority of the most "conservative" voters in the state of Vermont consistently vote to elect a socialist congressman?

Somehow, in the process of taking over the national Democratic Party, the DLC has not been required to demonstrate why the party should change its policies to meet voters' self-identification, rather than to embrace policies endorsed by a vast majority of Americans. This failure cannot be taken lightly, particularly when it comes to energizing young people. Without a core set of beliefs, young people will continue to bypass elections or vote third party. And no movement has survived in this country without young people.

This takes us to the next point.

How About Less Appealing and More Being?

During any national election cycle, our newspapers are filled daily with stories of campaign stops to "appeal" to women, IT leaders, investors, or the like. Maybe the candidate for president has discovered that single professional women might tip the election in one direction and so he schedules a meeting with that demographic in a swing state.

Younger people like myself can understand the importance

of getting the message to different types of voters. But we also understand the nature of a chameleon, and we don't want to vote for a leaf and elect a reptile. Over the last ten years, the Republican Party has aggressively staked out positions on issues of importance, while the Democrats have slumped along like a kid brother, following the general formula of proposing half of everything bad and double everything good.

I will leave it to professionals to argue the psychology of elections or congressional strategy. But as a voter, and since you've been losing elections, I hope you will leave it to me to tell you that voters are tiring of "the man of a thousand faces." The Republicans are publicly consistent, and voters know—at least they think they do—what to expect from them. Perhaps most alarming of all, at the university level campus activists are increasingly likely to look like George Will rather than, well, an improvement on that.

What's a Party to Do?

The Democratic Party needs to reaffirm its party platform. John Podesta recently said about the Democratic Party: "The one thing that unites us is, to some extent, negative—we're united in thinking that the Republicans are wrong." That is not good enough anymore. The Republicans being wrong doesn't make the Democrats right. Even many Gore voters, for instance, admitted that Nader was "more right" than their candidate on many issues.

Such a reaffirmation could take the form of a Contract with America–like agenda, a more united stand against the current administration, or an energetic issue-based convention.

The way to enforce this new code or set of party beliefs is with the one thing that all politicians understand—money. There is room in the Democratic Party (or any other) for debate. Not every candidate need be identical, and ideological discussion among allies helps build a strong, relevant party. But frankly, when someone drifts too far from the core, they're probably in the wrong party. The national party, then, should not commit any national funds to candidates who do not commit their support to a core set of principles. Then the Democratic Party will find its ranks energized and, having shed the last of the invisible clothes, the emperor can don something vibrant so long in the waiting.

Giving Life to
the Declaration of Intent

Ambassador Carol Moseley Braun

An attorney and business consultant practicing in Chicago, CAROL MOSELEY BRAUN is a candidate for the Democratic nomination for president of the United States. She has served as ambassador to New Zealand and Samoa (1999–2001); as United States senator from Illinois (1992–1998); as Cook County recorder of deeds and registrar of titles (1988–1992); as assistant majority leader and state representative (1978–1988); and as assistant United States attorney for the Northern District of Illinois (1973–1977). She is a graduate of the University of Chicago Law School (J.D. 1972) and the University of Illinois (B.A. 1968).

She is the mother of one son, Matthew, twenty-five, a computer engineer.

MAY 29, 2003

WHEN I WAS AMBASSADOR TO NEW ZEALAND, I WAS HONORED TO be embraced by the native Maori people and made an honorary member of the Te Atiawa tribe. The Maori, who populated the Pacific Islands from Tahiti to Samoa, have a fascinating history and a very instructive ancient philosophy.

The Maori see the relationship between the past, the present, and the future differently than we do. We see the future as before us, the glorious days yet to come, and we see the past as behind us, as that which is done and over. The Maori see it just the opposite. To them, the past is what stands before you. It is what you know. It is what you have experienced. It is what has stood the test of time. The future, on the other hand, is seen by Maori as standing behind you. It is mysterious, it is unknown, it is what you cannot see. This reversal of perspective can have a profound effect.

The most compelling aspect of this view is what it says about the present. With the past in front of us, providing us with guidance, the future will be that which we create by our actions in present time. We can't see the future, but it will be the result of what we do today. The future is the legacy we leave from our actions today. If we allow that which has gone before to illuminate our actions in the present time, the future we create will be better than the reality we inherit. We look to the past not out of nostalgia, but to better fulfill our responsibilities to our children.

Americans have always been a hopeful people who anticipate progress. We refer with great reverence to our fundamental political compacts, written in another time but describing core cultural values that continue to be embraced by all of us: *We hold these Truths to be self-evident, that all Men are created equal, that they are endowed by their Creator with certain unalienable Rights, that among these are Life, Liberty, and the Pursuit of Happiness*. . . . The unfortunate truth is, as Dr. Martin Luther King once put it, the Declaration of Independence should have been named the Declaration of Intent. The Founding Fathers certainly wrote truths, but those truths were far from self-evident when they were made part of our national political compact. Indeed, when the Constitution was written, neither women nor the poor were allowed to vote, and blacks were counted as three-fifths of a person for purposes of the census. The vast majority of the population was relegated to a limited set of roles that were defined for them by their station in life, and human potential and capacity were almost exclusively defined by the accident of one's birth. A republic had been created; democracy was a stretch of the imagination.

Our national character has been defined over time by our efforts to live up to the noble intent of that declaration and promise, and our progress has been reflected in the extent to which we have liberated human capacity through the inclusion and sharing of the blessings of liberty with all Americans.

We have moved as a nation in fits and starts in the direction of the core values of our Declaration of Intent. If we look at our past, it reflects a gradual, albeit not always linear, expansion of the reality of liberty. To the extent that we make the promise real, transform the intent into action, we will move our country closer to the Founding Fathers' noble vision.

Each generation has been challenged to rededicate and redefine that vision in ways that reflect its times and its realities. Each generation is confronted with its own humanity in ways that have ramifications and meaning for generations to follow.

And so, while the civil rights movement of the 1950s and '60s was ostensibly about race, it was also about repudiating hypocrisy and affirming the morality of our social order. It was an essentially patriotic movement that sought to make America live up to its highest and most noble ideals. It was a movement of liberation that had as its full reference the core values embraced by all Americans. It moved us to reach for those self-evident truths, and in so doing took our country closer to the morality of its most fundamental values.

It is to that history of struggle, the fight to expand the blessings of liberty and the moral high ground seized by our ancestors, that we must look as we take up the new challenges of our times. The Founding Fathers started a movement to liberate a country based on the liberation of the human spirit. We are still engaged in a struggle to give life to the nobility of their vision.

A nation that taps the talents of 100 percent of its people is a stronger nation. No true meritocracy, or democracy, can exist if the capacity to contribute is constrained by gender. Freedom is not a zero-sum game. The empowerment of women lifts others, and America stands poised to benefit from the added energy and talent, creativity and humanity, that women bring to civil society.

The empowerment of women is therefore not just a matter of self-interest for those of us who are female; it is a matter of national interest for all Americans. The time has come to shift the debate to focus not only on the rights of the individual to contribute to the maximum extent of his or her potential, but on the benefit to society in having access to all the talent and possibilities available to it.

Diversity stirs the talent pool, and all Americans benefit from an expansion of opportunity. The self-interest of men is therefore intimately wrapped up in the status of women. Patriotism in our time requires that the men of America look to and promote the empowerment of women, so that together we can remove the barriers to opportunity and achievement that limit national capacity.

The concept of individual liberty, radical as it was in the 1700s, remains a radical notion today. A society whose respect for the spirit of each person is its reason for being cannot long labor under the weight of discrimination based on biology. As our generation grapples with inclusion, we do so in light of the fights for freedom that have preceded us, and in anticipation of the predicate for justice our decisions will establish.

Social justice, diversity, tolerance, creativity, and freedom, these are all virtues that can be found at the heart of our national character. Our fundamental political compacts are given life by the extent to which these national virtues continue to prevail, and to the extent that the blessings of liberty continue to be spread to all people.

Progress is not linear. It rarely moves in a straight line. As progress is achieved, it becomes the predicate for reaction to it. The challenge is always to move from point to point in the direction of the ideals and virtues of our national character and to give life to the intent of our fundamental political compacts. The Maori would counsel us to look to the continuing thread of our past, to the triumphs as well as the setbacks that have brought us where we are today, and to understand that our actions in present time are simply creating our generation's legacy to the future.

How Mary Landrieu
Won Louisiana

Professor Douglas Brinkley

DOUGLAS BRINKLEY *is a professor of history and the director of the Eisenhower Center for American History at the University of New Orleans. He has written biographies of Franklin D. Roosevelt, Jimmy Carter, Dean Acheson, Rosa Parks, and James Forrestal. His latest book is* Wheels for the World: Henry Ford, His Company, and a Century of Progress 1903–2003.

"I been to Sugar Town, I shook the sugar down."

—Bob Dylan

WHEN RECALLING ELECTION NIGHT 2002, SENATOR MARY LAN-drieu (D-LA) referred to a singular state of being: shock. Channel surfing between CNN, ABC, and NBC, the incumbent Landrieu learned that she had failed to win an outright majority in her state's antiquated "open primary" election. She had been one of nine candidates from all parties on the November 5 ballot. And even though Landrieu had won 46 percent of the vote she had failed to hit the 50 percent mark. Therefore, according to Louisiana law, she was forced to enter a runoff slated for December 7 against the top Republican candidate, challenger Suzanne Haik Terrell, who had netted only 27 percent of the vote.

The evening grew even darker for Landrieu as the dismal election returns came trickling in from Missouri, Minnesota, and Georgia—all states she had assumed would reelect their Democratic senatorial candidates. Television commentators dubbed the election "Black Tuesday" for Democrats—friends of Landrieu were losing everywhere. The GOP was making a clean sweep. "I had been so focused on my race that I didn't follow the dynamics of others too closely," Landrieu recalled. "But when I got the news that both Max Cleland and Roy Barnes lost in Georgia my knees buckled. They were moderate Southern Democrats like myself. For a flashing second I thought that maybe I too was doomed. But I quickly pulled myself together. My disappointment turned to rage as I learned how conservative Republicans had tarnished the reputation of a great Vietnam War patriot like Max Cleland. My insides turned steely. This anger helped me prepare for December 7. I was going to win."

And win Landrieu did—quite decisively. She garnered 52 percent of the vote compared to Terrell's 48 percent. Her reelection punctured the conservative myth that the Democratic Party should concede the South forever to the Republicans. Despite Herculean efforts by the Bush administration and other conservatives, the Democrats in Louisiana held on to a Senate seat and also gained a GOP-held congressional seat. Nobody, however, would argue that post-1968 life is easy for Democrats in the South. But a Democrat with the right moderate message and independent personality *can* win. It's worth remembering that since 1994 the Democrats have won either a U.S. Senate seat or governorship in Florida, Georgia, Mississippi, Alabama, South Carolina, North Carolina, Kentucky, Arkansas, Louisiana, and Tennessee—every Southern state except Texas. "Tonight a great light has gone on in the United States because we turned the lights on," Landrieu said at her Fairmont Hotel victory party in New Orleans. "The light has shown that the Democratic Party is alive and well and united."

That was quite a statement by Landrieu. Ever since September 11, 2001, when two jetliners crashed into the World Trade Center, another plane struck the Pentagon, and another burst into flames in a Pennsylvania field, the Democratic Party has become rudderless. A full year after the horror of 9/11 Democrats were still paranoid that any negative critique of the Bush administration would be interpreted as unpatriotic. Their collective post–9/11 goal, it seemed, with the notable exception of a few mavericks, like Senator Robert Byrd of West Virginia, was to *behave well*. This is hardly leadership. Very few Democrats, for example, thought the so-called Bush Doctrine—which called for military action against potential enemies amassing weapons of mass destruction—was a legitimate long-range policy initiative, but few spoke up. They were scared. Dissent wasn't a politically expedient posture. All the Bush administration had to do was wave the flag and watch the Democrats cower.

Momentum is an important part of American politics, and the Republicans had clearly seized the high ground. As the 2002 midterm elections approached, doing only what might assure their own survival became the Democratic Party's modus operandi instead of striving for victory. Like a raisin in the sun, unable to take the heat, the Democratic Party shrank in stature, reacting instead of initiating. Days before the election, the Democrats offered no Kennedyesque images of candidates rolling up their shirtsleeves for the working class (or even Clintonian moments about feeling the electorate's pain). Instead we got toothless candidates in a defensive crouch, afraid of being stampeded by elephants. They failed to find a wedge issue—something Landrieu did at a local level in Louisiana.

As the Democratic Party prepares for the 2004 election, it's worth contemplating what the Landrieu campaign—unlike many others—did right following Black Tuesday. It must be stated from the outset that Landrieu—the daughter of former New Orleans mayor and Carter administration secretary of Housing and Urban Development Moon Landrieu—ran against a weak candidate. Suzanne Haik Terrell, known for her trademark haughtiness, turned condescending and snide. Her big campaign boast was that she was close to George W. Bush, and she bragged that she voted with the president 90 percent of the time. She ran on the notion that Louisiana already had one Democratic senator—John Breaux—and now the state needed a loyal Republican in Washington, D.C., to get things done. The highlight of her campaign occurred when President Bush campaigned for her in Shreveport and New Orleans, raising over $1 million for her. Since Bush carried the state in 2000 and had an approximately 65 percent favorable rating in Louisiana polls, Terrell wrapped herself around the White House like a patriotic banner on the Fourth of July. In addition to President Bush, a parade of other Republicans came to Louisiana to stump for Terrell, including former president George Bush, Vice President Dick Cheney, former New York City mayor Rudy Giuliani, and incoming Senate Majority Leader Trent Lott.

With great fortitude and grit, Landrieu challenged this Terrell–Bush–National GOP coalition head-on. Starting on November 6 Landrieu began preparing for battle against Terrell. She made a few key independent decisions that served her well. First, she was determined not to let the opposition smear her reputation. She directly challenged every insult and innuendo hurled her way. "More firepower," she kept telling herself. "A strong offense and a strong defense. This was war." With the help of three U.S. senators—Harry Reid (D-NV), Tom Daschle (D-SD), and John Breaux (D-LA)—she quickly raised some money from the Democratic caucus. But then she made the decision that saved her senatorial seat—she asked so-called national Democrats, with the important exception of the Black Caucus, to stay out of Louisiana. She didn't want to be seen jogging with Bill Clinton or visiting wetlands with Al Gore or praying at a synagogue with Joe Lieberman. "I didn't need to bring Big Names into the state to win," she recalled. "I needed to prove that I was an independent voice." While Terrell was bragging that she was essentially a rubber stamp for President Bush, Landrieu kept telling voters she was her own woman, a true independent who always put "Louisiana First."

Over the years Landrieu had become fed up with the so-called Beltway syndrome. She was appalled at how the gregarious Terry McAuliffe types kept selling a National Democratic Message for all fifty states. Somehow the DNC had lost sight of the first rule of electoral warfare: all politics is local. What played well in Kansas or California or Maine did not necessarily play well in Louisiana. Her party's top consultants, however, were trying to sanitize her message. "I balked at the DNC message machine," Landrieu recalled. "Their approach might work for presidential candidates but in Louisiana you need an independent, issue-by-issue approach."

Determined to do things her own way, Landrieu's next decision was to quickly solidify her base. "I didn't run away from gay-lesbian *or* Christian organizations," she recalled. "I embraced them and started coalition building." She had to reinvigorate her Democratic base. To do so Landrieu had to distance herself from President Bush, even though she had previously noted that she had voted with him 74 percent of the time. She made it clear that when it came to economic matters, civil rights issues, and environmental standards she would oppose the president head-on. She clearly understood that in order to win the runoff election a large African-American turnout was necessary. "Voters may like George Bush and support quite a few of his policies, but the reality is they don't want someone who's going to follow any party's doctrine," Senator John Breaux explained about the Landrieu victory strategy. "The tide at least has been stopped, this idea that the president can just go anywhere and work magic."

By becoming a Bush-bashing old-style Democrat, Landrieu invigorated her campaign. Many yellow-dog Democrats who stayed home on November 5 were now proud to pull a lever for Landrieu on December 7. A shrewd Landrieu agreed with what Harold Meyerson wrote in *The American Prospect*: the Democrats had no message to sell on November 5. "They were an opposition party that drew no lines of opposition," he wrote. "They had nothing to say. And on Tuesday, their base responded by staying home in droves." Or as fellow Louisianan James Carville put it: "We've got to stand *for* something. No one made the case." To her credit Landrieu had learned the fundamental lesson of the midterm election: Democrats were not going to get elected by not criticizing George W. Bush.

Since she agreed with much of Bush's post–9/11 foreign policy, Landrieu desperately needed a kinetic statewide issue— besides defending Social Security—that would differentiate her from the Terrell-Bush platform. That's when the sugar issue fell from the sky and landed in her lap, via a November 20 report in the Mexican newspaper *Reforma* that claimed a secret trade deal had been struck between George Bush and Vicente Fox, the president of Mexico. The heart of the issue was whether Mexico should be allowed to ship 300,000 metric tons of displaced sugar into the United States in 2003. News of this "secret Mexican sugar deal" angered Louisiana farmers, who already had an anti-NAFTA bent. "The deal, if it exists, could dramatically shrink or even destroy the Louisiana sugar industry," declared Brian Breaux, sugar specialist for the Louisiana Farm Bureau Federation. "At this time, representatives of the American Sugar Cane League are actively urging the U.S. Trade Representative (USTR) to Mexico to quash any deal which could devastate the U.S. sugar industry."

With great zeal Landrieu seized upon this obscure Mexican newspaper story, making it the centerpiece of her reelection campaign. She rightfully claimed that the secret deal to import Mexican sugar would hinder the livelihood of twenty-seven thousand Louisiana sugarcane farmers. Due to bad weather Louisiana's sugar growers were already having a hard time. The White House plan to double Mexican sugar imports was just another cruel and callous blow. Even Republican governor Foster admitted that such a deal would destroy his party in Louisiana for a generation. In the critical Acadian area of the state, where sugar is king, Terrell had been polling quite well. Landrieu and her troops, many waving ten-foot stalks of sugarcane as if they were pitchforks, went on a brutal offensive. At rally after rally in Cajun country, Landrieu claimed that she put "Louisiana First" while Terrell was the trained poodle of President Bush, a rubber stamp who disdained working-class people. "The sugar issue crystallized what I was saying," Landrieu explained. "Sometimes a president's policies are wrong for a state. That's just the way it is. . . . It was powerful out there."

If the Democratic Party hopes to regain either the U.S. Senate or the House of Representatives, its candidates must learn the Landrieu lessons: don't be afraid to criticize the Bush administration; solidify your base; immediately respond to ad hominem attacks by an opponent; deviate, when necessary, from the DNC line (i.e., refuse to march in lockstep with Terry McAuliffe); don't be afraid to cut taxes (Democratic governor Bill Richardson did so and watched his popularity soar); ignore Beltway lobbyists and find a heated local issue to embrace as your own. And, at all times, be forceful. The wimp factor usually spells doom for the Democratic candidate. "When people feel insecure," Bill Clinton correctly advised fellow Democrats after Black Tuesday, they prefer "somebody who's strong and wrong than somebody who's weak and right." Recapping the December 7 runoff election in Louisiana, syndicated columnist E. J. Dionne perfectly summed up why Landrieu defeated Terrell: toughness. "When President Bush threw everything except poisoned gumbo into the fight to defeat Landrieu in Saturday's runoff, she didn't fold," he wrote. "She hit Bush where it hurts on the economics, and threw sugar in his eyes. She told the voters in a very pro-Bush state that they had a choice between a Bush rubber-stamp or an independent voice. Independence beat Bush."

The Middle:
Where the Work Gets Done

Congressman Mike Castle

A former deputy attorney general, state legislator, lieutenant governor, and two-term governor of Delaware, MIKE CASTLE is currently serving his sixth term as Delaware's sole member in the U.S. House of Representatives. Focusing his efforts on finding pragmatic, bipartisan solutions to some of the most pressing problems facing the nation, he is a leader of the House Tuesday Group, an organization of centrist House Republicans who meet weekly to discuss policy issues and influence legislation.

OUR NATION IS DRAMATICALLY DIFFERENT THAN IT WAS BEFORE September 11, 2001. There is no question that what is important to the American people, and how that translates into priorities for our nation, has been dramatically impacted by the events of the past two years. The terrorist attacks and their immediate aftermath were certainly a factor in the 2002 elections, not because most politicians explicitly campaigned on the issue, but because of what the average American was feeling. All Americans in some way were affected by the heinous attacks on our nation, and consequently became more focused on their safety and security. Immediately following September 11, a renewed sense of American pride in our country, and in our commitment to one another, swept across the nation. Americans also increased their focus on the president's leadership and the role of Congress and the federal government.

Following September 11, it appears that most Americans wanted the federal government and their elected representatives to work together to improve our homeland security and to fight terrorism. These policy priorities have also undeniably affected the political landscape in which our elections were conducted. When the nation experiences an external challenge, Americans generally rally around their president and their government.

One outcome of the terrorist attacks is that Americans are more focused on their government. It is a renewed realization that one of our Constitution's fundamental duties for the federal government is to "provide for the common defense" of our nation. With the new and varied threats presented by terrorism, this involves not only our military, but also the many aspects of homeland security. Americans want the government to address problems of concern to them in an efficient manner, but they retain the traditional American view that they do not want the government controlling their lives. Republicans and Democrats alike must draw lessons from this.

Both political parties must adapt to these changed circumstances and the new political environment. The party that is seen as actually addressing the concerns of Americans directly and responsibly during these uncertain times will have the clear electoral advantage for the foreseeable future. At this point, Republicans have the advantage, but both political parties must make adjustments in their approach to win the consistent confidence of the American people.

Political labels seem to matter much more in Washington than they do at the state and local levels. I have become convinced that most Americans view themselves as generally centrist or moderate, as being in the middle of the political spectrum. Both major political parties must recognize that the American people want an efficient government to address the problems of concern to them without wasting their money. The parties should start with a positive message. Voters will ultimately respond to the candidates who best communicate the message that they are trying to address voters' concerns. Elected officials succeed best when they appeal to the needs and common sense of Americans first, and resist partisanship and name-calling as much as possible. Genuine differences exist between candidates and between parties and they should not be denied, but voters can sense when candidates pursue ideological battles over real solutions, which often involve compromise.

President George W. Bush has broad support among Americans because he has taken decisive action to address the terrorist threat. But he has also been successful because he has made issues like improving public education a priority. Improving public schools and ensuring that children from every ethnic and economic background have the chance to succeed is a priority for voters across the political spectrum. President Clinton succeeded when he pursued centrist policies like welfare reform and balancing the federal budget. Both parties drive independents and their own moderate party members away when they appear to be driven by the more extreme special interests.

Moderates in both parties are critical to the future success of our political system because they reflect the views of the majority of Americans. Moderates focus on finding solutions and enacting legislation that solves problems, rather than creating arguments that may make for entertaining cable talk shows but don't do much to help Americans.

As a moderate Republican, I urge our party to act in the spirit of Lincoln and Theodore Roosevelt. Like Lincoln we must always stand first and foremost for opportunity and freedom for every American. Like Teddy Roosevelt, we must be for honest and fair business practices and for protecting our environment. We must be stewards of the taxpayers' dollars, spend them wisely on genuine needs, and reduce taxes when possible. But just as a government program is not the solution to every problem, neither is a tax cut a magical solution to every economic challenge. Fiscal responsibility and balancing budgets inspire confidence in financial markets and working Americans.

I have consistently argued that Americans want their government to advance public policies that reflect a limited but responsible role for government. These policies should be shaped to realize economic growth, fiscal responsibility, and a nation that is truly secure and globally competitive.

Obviously, as the party in power at this time, the president and congressional Republicans bear the ultimate responsibility for effective and successful governing. However, there is also significant pressure on the Democrats to communicate practical policy alternatives that are not simply based on stirring up fear among different segments of the population. Republicans cannot fall back on outdated tactics such as attacking the federal government as the root of all problems. Americans realize that the world we face requires a strong international policy and our domestic problems are complex and nationwide, demanding a role for the federal government. Democrats cannot resort to class warfare or soak-the-rich arguments. All Americans want to succeed economically; pitting workers against business owners or lower-income brackets against upper is part of the politics of the past.

American voters continue to seek candidates who can articulate issues and results that address their primary concerns, including economic and educational opportunities.

Our government faces very great international challenges that go to the very core of our nation—its safety and security against foreign threats. Combating terrorism and a war to disarm Iraq are the top policy priorities for us. However, very close behind is the need to revitalize the economy and face the domestic challenges of our nation. The 2004 elections will undoubtedly be about whether we have preserved our national security and righted the economy. The time before the next election will be the fundamental test of national and international leadership for President Bush and his administration. Without question, a complete end of terrorist threats will not be realized in the next year, but Americans will judge whether progress is being made.

Americans want results. They don't expect perfect solutions to difficult problems, but they want honest efforts to address their concerns. Finger-pointing and partisanship don't go very far among people in my state of Delaware or the rest of the nation. Moderate positions may not get many headlines, but centrist efforts to find compromises and solutions are essential to establishing a record of accomplishment on virtually every issue from national security to the economy, health care, education, and transportation.

We have much work to do to protect our homeland and get our economy moving again. The center is where most Americans are. Both parties need to realize that. In my own party, moderate Republicans should redouble their efforts to craft centrist, bipartisan solutions to the challenges facing our country. It may not make for the boldest headlines or dramatic direct-mail appeals, but the middle is where the work gets done.

It's Not the Economy, Stupid

Linda Chavez

LINDA CHAVEZ is the president of the Center for Equal Opportunity in Sterling, Virginia, and the author of An Unlikely Conservative: The Transformation of an Ex-Liberal *(Basic Books, 2002). She writes a syndicated newspaper column and is a Fox News Channel contributor. She served as director of public liaison in the Reagan White House and as director of the U.S. Commission on Civil Rights from 1983 to 1985. In 1986, Chavez was the Republican nominee for U.S. senator from Maryland.*

WITH THE PRESIDENTIAL ELECTION BARELY EIGHTEEN MONTHS away, the Democrats are hoping a weak economy will give them a chance to win back the White House. It worked in 1992, when Bill Clinton defeated the popular George Herbert Walker Bush, who had driven Saddam Hussein out of Kuwait but seemed clueless about how to respond to the relatively mild recession that followed the Gulf War. Clinton operatives summed up their entire, winning strategy in one phrase: "It's the economy, stupid." Now a new batch of Democratic contenders are hoping they can convince Americans it's still the economy—but voters have gotten a lot smarter.

The American economy is so large—more than $10 trillion—there's very little any president can do to stimulate economic growth and create jobs in the short run. President Reagan—who had the largest impact on the economy of any recent president—cut taxes, encouraged the Federal Reserve Board to keep interest rates high in order to bring down inflation, and slowed the growth of government spending on domestic programs. But even Reagan was only partly responsible for the tremendous expansion in the economy that began during his tenure and has continued to the present. Stable oil prices helped keep inflation low. The advent of corporate raiders forced American companies to stay lean and mean. The influx of immigrant workers and the relative weakness of American labor unions kept inflationary wage increases in check. The expansion of free trade policies in markets around the world and the explosion in technology also contributed to a healthy U.S. economy through the 1990s until now.

Bill Clinton, who is credited with presiding over a robust economy for eight years, succeeded more because of what he couldn't accomplish than anything he actually did. In his first year in office, Clinton tried to nationalize some 7 percent of the U.S.

economy with Hillary's health care proposal and, luckily, failed. He increased government spending, but only modestly, thanks to the Republican takeover of Congress in 1994. He raised taxes, but only once—which nonetheless explains why the economy grew at a slower rate in the 1990s compared to the boom period between 1982 and 1990. Had Clinton succeeded at the usual Democratic interventionist economic policies, his tenure would have been a huge bust.

George W. Bush inherited an economy that had already started into a cyclical downturn, which the terrorist attacks of 9/11 only made worse. There is little indication, however, that the American public blames President Bush. Although the economy grew at a sluggish 1.6 percent in the first quarter of 2003, other economic indicators are healthy. Interest rates are at historic lows; inflation is modest; consumer confidence is up; and energy prices, which had been rising, are coming back down again. The best thing President Bush can do for the economy is to ignore Democratic cries to fix it.

With its size and complexity, there is no way to jump-start the U.S. economy with government stimulus packages or other quick-fix gimmicks. President Bush's goal should be to make long-term adjustments that will allow businesses to thrive and encourage ordinary Americans to save and invest. With a closely divided Congress, it's unlikely the president will be able to win support for some of the most important changes that would affect the permanent health of the economy—the elimination of capital gains taxes and a sizable reduction in marginal tax rates. Even moderate Republicans have resisted the president's full tax-cut proposal out of fear that budget deficits will grow uncontrollably.

Of course Republicans, who control both houses of Congress and the White House, could reduce the deficit by significantly cutting government spending—but neither the president nor GOP leaders in Congress are interested in that politically risky solution. Unlike most families, who tighten their belts and do without when faced with smaller paychecks, politicians seem unable to cut spending when there's a budget shortfall. Nonetheless, despite Democrats' hopes that the economy will nose-dive into a double-dip recession in the next few months, most economists predict that the economy will either continue to grow at its current modest rate or actually expand more rapidly over the next year. Either way, the voters are likely to give President Bush the benefit of the doubt on the economy and reelect him based on his leadership in fighting terrorism at home and abroad.

How Democrats Can Come Back

Honorable William J. Clinton

WILLIAM J. CLINTON *is the forty-second president of the United States. He now heads the William J. Clinton Presidential Foundation, which works to fight HIV/AIDS; for racial, religious, and ethnic reconciliation; economic empowerment of the poor; and citizen service.*

IS THE DEMOCRATIC PARTY DEAD? SINCE LAST YEAR'S ELECTIONS, a lot of people have been saying that. But I respectfully disagree. We heard that back in 1991. It was wrong then, and it's wrong now.

It's true that Democrats didn't have a good year in 2002. We didn't run the best political campaign in our history. Republicans beat us on message, money, and turnout. And, to a lot of Democrats and independents, we were missing in action when it came to the issue that matters most today—national security.

Without a strong position on national security, Democrats won't be listened to on other issues. We cannot overestimate the psychological impact of September 11. Pulling together after the attacks, the American people felt a deep need for unity and strength. When people feel uncertain, they would rather have somebody who's wrong and strong than somebody who is weak and right.

That's why Democrats bear just as heavy a responsibility to unite the nation on national security as does the party in the White House. We need a national message that says where we agree and disagree with the Republicans, one that defends our record and offers positive proposals for the future. Our record is strong: Democrats have been virtually unanimous in supporting the fight against terror and additional defense spending to get it done. Most Democrats have supported the president on Iraq. They've said yes to unlimited inspections and the use of force if the United Nations resolution is not honored. And the Homeland Security bill was Senator Joe Lieberman's proposal, one that the Bush administration opposed for seven months.

But we failed to get that message out, or to emphasize our party's ideas for achieving greater national security.

One key to national security is accountability. Clearly someone needs to be accountable for intelligence sharing and for law enforcement. Even within the new Department of Homeland Security, there must be clear lines of communication so that we can avoid the kinds of bureaucratic problems we faced before September 11, when there were reports of people learning to fly airplanes without learning takeoffs and landings, but no one checked the roughly two thousand flight schools in America.

Accountability also means modernizing information technology. Mohammed Atta, the terrorist ringleader, had twelve addresses: two were residences; apparently ten were safe houses for his coconspirators. Another terrorist had thirty credit cards and $250,000 in debt. That information was in the computers of at least one, and probably more, of the mass-mailing companies in our country, along with similar information on all the rest of us. That's why modernizing our technology to share intelligence is such an important part of homeland security. If a person has been in our country just a year or two and already has several residences or large credit card debts, he is either very wealthy or up to no good. It shouldn't be too difficult to determine which is true.

Democrats have a stronger position on homeland security than Republicans. The administration can reorganize the government all it wants. But what is it doing to protect the tunnels, the bridges, the water systems, and the utilities? What is it doing to provide help for our first responders—police, firefighters, and emergency medical services? What is it doing to help those who must respond to an anthrax attack or a chemical weapons release? Democrats have pushed to provide adequate funding for these things against constant Republican resistance. These issues matter a lot more than which bureaucratic box you put things in. Yet we didn't get that message out in the elections.

Democrats should take the lead on another homeland security issue: energy independence. I tried unsuccessfully for three years to get the Republican Congress to produce tax credits for the production and purchase of energy conservation and clean energy products. There is a $1 trillion global market for these products, which will create jobs for Americans, fight global warming, and make us less dependent on volatile areas of the world. There is no excuse for not taking stronger action now, and Democrats should lead the way.

Besides homeland security, we need to do more about weapons of mass destruction. We're doing the right thing in Iraq, but we need to do more. We have a very dangerous situation in North Korea, which could turn itself into a nuclear assembly plant within months. This is not an issue that can wait on some back burner. We have to help our friends fight terror, from Colombia to the Philippines to Indonesia.

And we must do more to safeguard existing stockpiles of weapons of mass destruction. When I was president, we spent a lot of federal funds moving nuclear weapons out of Kazakhstan, Belarus, and Ukraine into Russia, where they could be secured and destroyed. We agreed with the Russians to destroy fifty tons of plutonium on each side. Thanks to the Nunn-Lugar legislation, in some years we also paid the salaries of about thirty thousand Russian scientists engaged in nuclear, chemical, or biological weapons production. By supporting them, we hoped they wouldn't be tempted, after six months without a paycheck, to go to work for someone who might do us harm. The Nunn-Lugar program has helped deactivate almost six thousand nuclear warheads and destroy approximately eight hundred nuclear missiles in Russia. The program has also helped secure approximately forty percent of Russia's vulnerable nuclear materials. We should extend Nunn-Lugar efforts to other nations with weapons of mass destruction and weapons-grade material, and we should emphasize biological and chemical as well as nuclear materials and programs. Congress declined to take these steps last year. Democrats should push for them early in 2003.

In the security arena, we also need a positive agenda to make more partners and fewer terrorists. We need to remember the Marshall Plan and the rebuilding of Japan. We need to boost foreign aid and debt relief. We need to make it possible for millions of kids who are not attending school to get an education. In the developing world, every year of mandatory schooling adds 10 to 15 percent to a person's annual income.

I recently helped the great Peruvian economist Hernando de Soto set up the Foundation for Building the Capital of the Poor in Ghana. The foundation helps move poor people's assets into the legal system so they can use them as collateral for credit, to improve their own lives and help grow their nation's economy. We should help more nations develop legal systems in which people have clear title to their homes, farms, and businesses and every incentive to be tax-paying members of society. There's a shirt factory in Ghana that exports to the United States under the African-Caribbean trade bill I signed. When I was leaving Ghana, a woman came running up to me at the airport and gave me one of the shirts. She thanked me for helping to make it possible for four hundred people to have jobs in that factory.

People like that don't become terrorists. They don't hate us; they like us. They don't want their kids fighting tribal wars or planting bombs in America. They don't resent our wealth, because they see that we want them to have it, too.

Once we Democrats have a comprehensive security plan in place, we can talk about the other key issues, such as the economy. Our economic plan is simple: we want economic growth for everybody. In the 1990s, we had 22 million new jobs compared with 14 million in the Reagan recovery. And we moved almost eight million people out of poverty—one hundred times as many as in the Reagan years. We also helped create more millionaires and billionaires than any previous administration. I never pass up a chance to remind my Republican friends how well they did under us. One of them recently said to me, "As a Republican, I voted against you twice. Now I wish you were back."

We Democrats are equal-opportunity prosperity folks. Among the biggest problems the country faces are the tax cuts that President Bush pushed through Congress. The administration insisted on passage of the tax cuts before anyone knew what our income was going to be, what our expenses were going to be, or what emergencies we might face. In fact, our income went down, our expenses went up, and we had a terrible emergency. Also, these tax cuts have too little stimulus in the short run and too little fiscal responsibility for the long run, with too many of the benefits going to the wealthiest Americans, who don't need them.

We should freeze the top tax rate on incomes of $400,000 and above, which affects only one-half of 1 percent of the taxpayers. We should raise the $1 million ceiling on the estate tax to $5 million per couple, but we should not get rid of it. Those two steps alone would save $1.4 trillion, including interest savings, over the next two decades. If we freeze the top two tax rates, including all incomes over $200,000, the savings jump to $2 trillion. That would make up around half the anticipated shortfall in the Social Security trust fund. Even with these freezes, by the way, a couple making $1 million a year would still get a $10,000 tax cut—more than ten times the amount the average American will get when the whole program is phased in. Democrats don't need to talk about repealing the tax cut or raising taxes—just about freezing the top rates.

The present path to long-term deficits isn't good for anyone. It means higher interest rates, weaker markets, fewer jobs, and reduced government support down the road for education, health care, the environment, and the poor.

Today, it means we're funding tax cuts for the wealthy by withholding funds from education and depleting the Social Security and Medicare trust funds. That's bad ethics, bad policy, and bad economics.

While restoring a measure of long-term fiscal responsibility, we should do more to stimulate the economy in the short run. There are many options, including the kind of investment incentives that Senator Lieberman, Senator John Edwards, and others have called for; progressive rebates for working people who will spend the money now; incentives to help build energy security through alternative clean-energy sources and new conservation technologies; and help for people who feel insecure about their retirements, so they can have more access to 401(k)–type plans. If we don't modify the tax cuts so that we have more investment-consumption incentives in the short run and greater fiscal responsibility over the long run, we're going to be in big trouble.

There is another reason why the estate tax should not be abolished: it would drastically undermine America's tradition of well-endowed philanthropies, which have contributed so much to the welfare of the nation. That's why some of the richest people in the world are opposed to repealing the estate tax, including Bill Gates and Warren Buffett.

Another important way to stimulate the economy, while reminding voters of Democratic leadership on high-tech matters, is to better target government research dollars. During my presidency, we invested about $1 billion in nanotechnology. There's no question that the sequencing of the human genome, coupled with the diagnostic capabilities of nanotechnology, will soon enable us to save hundreds of thousands—maybe millions—of lives. This will not only benefit those affected, but will have a huge positive effect on our economy.

We've also got to make some long-term reforms on a whole range of issues. One of them is health care. In 1993 and 1994, the Republicans and the health insurance companies performed reverse plastic surgery on my health care proposal. The victors always get to write the history. After the failure of comprehensive reform, we adopted an aggressive step-by-step approach that produced impressive results, including greater portability through the Kennedy-Kassebaum bill; immunization of 90 percent of our young children for the first time; groundbreaking advances in diabetes care and breast and prostate cancer screening; a huge increase in medical research investments; and the largest increase in children's coverage since Medicaid—the Children's Health Insurance Program, providing 4.3 million children with health care.

Unfortunately, the number of uninsured people is going up again, despite the fact that in the United States we spend more than any other country on health care—14 percent of our gross domestic product. Fully 3 percent of that is on administrative costs—a huge amount of money. By contrast, the administrative costs of Medicare are 1 percent of program costs. With our high-tech medical system, we have to expect that health care will cost about 11 percent of GDP. Think about the numbers: if we could reconcile the various interests and free up 2 percent or 3 percent of wasted GDP, we could provide health insurance to many of America's 41 million uninsured at a cost we could support without a backlash. We Democrats should also be thinking a lot about how to prevent people from losing their health insurance in difficult economic times like these.

We also need to take another look at our work and family agenda. We're the pro-family, pro-work party. That's why we supported the Children's Health Insurance Program and the Family and Medical Leave Act. Our positions were very effective in the 1990s with a lot of middle-class people who work in the New Economy. Now that most parents are working, we need to find new ways to expand unpaid family and medical leave, and to provide incentives for paid leave and for more flex-time. You can't call a society successful unless people feel they can work and raise their children—while doing a good job at both. The Bush administration wants to withdraw the option I gave states to use excess unemployment insurance funds to finance paid family leave, just as many states are considering doing it. We should fight to give them the chance.

Finally, Democrats should press hard on corporate accountability. We were able to get a strong bill passed in the last Congress, even though the Republicans opposed it until the very end. But since then, they've withheld the funding to make it work, and we should make that an issue in the new Congress. At the same time, however, we shouldn't kill the goose that laid the golden egg. Democrats should be pro-accountability and pro-business. After all, a lot of U.S. companies did a great job in the 1990s, including with their stock options. But to avoid future Enrons, perhaps stock options should be executable only over a longer period of time—that would build employee loyalty and company strength. And it might prevent more people with inside knowledge from simply taking the money and running, leaving the other stockholders high and dry.

While putting a clear and strong Democratic program in place—robust national security combined with progressive domestic reforms—we must remember our basic beliefs. Democrats win with vision, values, and ideas. We must remind people that we're committed to a global community of peace, prosperity, freedom, and security. Martin Luther King, Jr., said the arc of the moral universe is long, but it bends toward justice. And the people who are the benders toward justice have the heavier burden. We chose to be Democrats. Nobody made us do it. We made that decision because we're committed to those values. If we honor those values and push the new ideas we believe in, Democrats will win elections again.

This article was adapted from a speech given to the Democratic Leadership Council in New York City on December 3, 2002. It first appeared in the January/February 2003 issue of "Blueprint," the policy journal of the Democratic Leadership Council.

Can Happy Days Be Here Again?

Richard Cohen

RICHARD COHEN *is a nationally syndicated columnist for* The Washington Post *who has been covering politics since 1968.*

AMONG THE SHOCKING MEMORIES OF MY BOYHOOD—THE SUDden death of Franklin D. Roosevelt, for instance—was my encounter with Emanuel Gerstein, who lived on my block and was unique among my parents' friends because he had gone to college. I was in the fifth or sixth grade, returning from school, when I bumped into Manny, who was also on his way home. Naturally, we discussed politics, about which I was precociously opinionated, when Manny offered the most astounding confession: he was a Republican.

I was stunned. In all of Far Rockaway, Queens, I knew no Republicans. They lived "out there" somewhere, beyond Queens, beyond New York City itself, and didn't drink milk from the container, but from a pitcher, as did Robert Young's family in *Father Knows Best*. They were the oddest of people.

That feeling of oddness stuck with me. When, some years later, Eisenhower defeated Stevenson (1952), I awoke the next morning expecting my world to be radically changed. I felt a sense of dread, as if aliens had come from outer space (or Ohio!), and somehow things would never again be the same. I was not exactly scared, but definitely on the alert. I kept expecting something dramatic to happen—something to correspond to the dread in which Republicans were then held. They were not mere political opponents, but the enemy. Yet, in Far Rockaway, for some reason, nothing happened. Within a day, I had acclimated.

Now I find myself voting for the occasional Republican. The first, I think, was John Lindsay, who was really a Democrat anyway, but then came others and still others. Now, to tell you the truth, my allegiance is in play. I still consider myself a Democrat— I have never voted for a Republican presidential candidate—and when I am at Republican political events such as nominating conventions, I look around at the vast Wonder Breadness of the crowd and conclude, almost viscerally, "These are not my people."

Yet more and more I feel a similar sense of alienation at Democratic events. I am a union member myself, but I feel little sense of identification with organized labor. Too often, the vaunted working man seems only to want to work at taking money from my pocket. I get all weepy about the Civil Rights movement, but I loathe affirmative action, a remedy that exchanges one set of victims for another.

I am a feminist, but I cannot connect to the grievances of some of its more militant spokes . . . er, persons. I am pro-choice, but not unquestionably so—not if it means permitting unrestricted late-term abortions.

I approve of welfare, which is simply charity by another name, but I am no longer enamored of the poor. Too often, they are victims of their own culture, not "my" economic system, and I have no patience any longer with anyone who blames crime on the "system" and not on criminals. The system needs fixing, but criminals need jailing.

It seems I have become fairly typical. No party—either Republican or Democratic—has all that I want and both parties contain much of what I do not want. I am becoming more and more of an independent, the sort of voter who gave the New Hampshire Republican primary to John McCain and will, almost certainly, play a similar role for the Democrats in 2004. With no real contest in the GOP—or so it looks at the moment—both independents and moderate Republicans are likely to vote in the Democratic primary. Given the importance of the New Hampshire primary—and given the fact that independents outnumber both Democrats and Republicans—it just could be that the next Democratic presidential nominee will be chosen by Republicans and independents.

New Hampshire, though, is something of an anomaly, since

it allows independents to vote in either party's primary. That's usually not the case elsewhere, making it hard to tell precisely how many independents there are. The University of Michigan's National Election Studies estimate they comprise 36 percent of the electorate—up from 23 percent in 1952, the year Ike staged his unsettling coup.

A Democrat who could appeal to independents and moderate Republicans would not be a bad thing for the party. Trouble is, what works in New Hampshire may not work in Iowa. In that state's caucuses, independents can't vote. And the Democrats who do are invariably party activists, including a fair share of retirees. Iowa pushes candidates to the left—not necessarily a bad thing if we're talking social issues or Social Security, but not such a good thing if we're talking foreign policy or defense policy.

McCain's appeal to independents and, it has to be said, to the journalists who covered him, stemmed from his willingness to take on Washington's special interests. The problem for Democrats is that these special interests—unions, trial lawyers, and minorities whose grievances seem disproportionate to their injury—come to the fore in the primaries. It sometimes seems that a Democratic nominating convention collects people who have demands to make of the party—as if the party is not their own.

The Republican Party, too, has its parochial special interests. It, too, has segments that are always threatening to bolt if this or that plank is not kept (or inserted) in a platform that almost no one ever reads and almost everyone instantly forgets. But the party is unified in its outlook on foreign policy, taxes, and the role (if any) of government—so much so that it's possible to wrap them all up in fragment sentences: strong defense, minimal taxes, and very little government. Democrats, dealing as they do with the real world, have a harder time of it.

After FDR—and his annex, Truman—the GOP really found its voice on foreign policy and its extension, the (nonexistent) domestic communist threat. It was unambiguously anticommunist and, if I may say so, unambiguously pro-American as well. It harbored no doubts about the virtues of America and the evils of communism. It was without guilt when it came to its own country, robustly nonneurotic about the American mission—and, of course, willing to encourage or merely tolerate all sorts of abuses, including McCarthyism. The Democratic Party might contain elements that mused over American responsibility for the Cold War, American guilt, American complicity, but not the GOP. It was clean on that score.

Now, once again, the GOP is united behind a robust and possibly reckless foreign policy—but not the Democrats. Many of its presidential candidates may have voted for the congressional resolution authorizing George W. Bush to use force in Iraq, but the party's rank and file seems to be in disagreement. Especially in Iowa, but also in New Hampshire and elsewhere, the more liberal elements of the party will almost certainly tug the presidential candidates leftward—maybe far enough so that they will cease being acceptable to the vast middle of the American electorate.

Vietnam is a case in point. It hardly matters that the party's position has been vindicated by history—by, among others, that Vietnam veteran himself, John McCain. At that time, the American people rejected the party's approach and elected Richard Nixon in a landslide. His opponent, George McGovern, was a weak candidate who managed, despite an impeccable combat record in World War II and solid Midwestern credentials, to become the personification, even a caricature, of the antiwar movement. The electorate may not have liked the Vietnam War much, but it disliked the antiwar movement even more.

It's hard—and somewhat unfair—to generalize, but there was something about the peace movement that was about more than peace. It was also furious at America, blaming Vietnam not on anticommunism run amok or Wilsonian moralism misapplied to Southeast Asia, but on capitalism, imperialism, militarism—any sort of ism that implied America had gone into Vietnam not because it was misguided, but because it was just plain rotten. It's not that Democrats are not patriots: it's rather that they are patriots with an asterisk—a caveat, an explanation. They don't have a parent's love for a child, but rather a child's love for the parent: so many hurts; so many issues. Can't we talk first?

The grievances are often authentic (although sometimes not) and, no matter what the case, historically based. Who can deny African Americans their history? Who can tell women they don't have a beef? Who can tell the poor that they and the rich play by the same rules—and on a wonderfully level field? Not me.

On the other hand, someone has to tell them that they are Americans first and members of a special, narrow constituency second. Someone—some candidate—has to tell them that there are causes greater than their narrow ones, that they are part of the whole and not the whole thing. If those words echo McCain's New Hampshire battle cry, they are meant to. By being a fiscal conservative and appearing a social liberal (or at least a rebel)—

by vowing to eschew special interests—McCain became just the sort of candidate independents and Democrats such as myself were, and are, seeking.

The candidate who can tell important constituency groups of the Democratic Party to, well, "get over it" will be the candidate to march the party to victory. The candidate who bases his foreign policy in an unabashed love for America—who dwells on the promise of the future and not the mistakes of the past—will in a significant way be returning the Democratic Party to the one of my childhood. I await, I yearn for, a Happy Warrior. I think the whole country does.

No One to Vote For

Sean "P. Diddy" Combs

Entertainment impresario SEAN "P. DIDDY" COMBS *is a multi-platinum recording artist, Grammy-winning producer, and business mogul. As founder and CEO of Bad Boy Entertainment, one of the world's preeminent urban entertainment companies, Combs is renowned as both an artist and an entrepreneur. Combs's corporate enterprise includes Bad Boy Records, the Sean John clothing line, Blue Flame Marketing and Advertising, Justin's restaurant, and his own charity, Daddy's House Social Programs, Inc.*

YOUNG PEOPLE DON'T VOTE. IT'S SAD TO HEAR THAT, BUT IT'S true. Young people just don't get out there to the polls in the numbers they should. They realize not voting is going to keep them frustrated and without power. The problem is that *there's no one to vote for.* Republicans and Democrats speak a good game—when asked about what they're doing to appeal to young people they'll spit chapter and verse about their record on education and social services—but in reality, politicians have given up on the kids. And so, in return, kids have given up on them.

The facts are there: even by inflated U.S. Census figures, voter turnout among eighteen- to twenty-four-year-olds has dropped in presidential elections over the past thirty years (the one big exception being Clinton in '92). It's been claimed that participation is as low as 40 percent, and that's only counting the kids who are eligible. The hundreds of thousands of young people locked up don't count. Neither do any convicted felons. And if it's not a presidential election, don't expect *any* young people to hit that polling booth. For what? To elect someone who's gonna be all talk? To elect someone who's not going to make any changes to affect day-to-day life? To elect someone who's not going to care about me at all, in any way?

This mentality runs rampant through the minds of young people, both black and white, rich and poor. It doesn't matter if you live in the 'hood or the suburbs. Nine times out of ten, you're going to believe—most of the time with good reason—that politics, *and politicians,* do not exist to serve any of your best interests. This is why young people feel so disenfranchised. And this is why the Democratic Party needs a big wake-up call. First, they have to be honest enough to admit that there is a problem. Then they need to figure out a way of doing something about it. What can be done to win the hearts and votes of young people in this country?

I believe you really need to know about and to whom it is you're talking. Whether it's an eighteen-year-old trying to find his/her first real job, or a twenty-two-year-old single parent. Someone fresh out of college, or a kid struggling to get off the street. You have to understand how those different individuals think and what they need. Know what they respect. If you're going to talk around them or above them, it's not going happen. If you're going to assume that they're stupid or not capable of understanding what the important issues are, then you're wrong again. And they'll smell you coming. No one is better at identifying someone who doesn't respect them than a young person who's been disrespected his/her whole life. Some phony politician, who knows nothing about my life or my struggle and comes around once in a while looking for my vote, I can see a mile away. What do you think, I'm going to give you my vote just because you pretend to care for me? You're gonna get my parents' vote because you think I'll tell them how cool you were to come to my block or school? That's not going to work either. I don't trust you.

In the black community, the problem is even worse. The disconnect between the politicians and the people is huge. I mean, to begin with, few white politicians are ever really going to understand what it's like to be a black man in America. How could they? They haven't spent nights in the 'hood with cockroaches crawling all over them. They don't get pulled over by the police every weekend. There are real reasons why our communities are so much worse when compared to similar white areas. Look at the parks, the train stations, the grocery stores. The garbage gets collected less often in my 'hood. There are far fewer jobs or good schools. Even the police cars are beat up.

Whether white or black, politicians never speak to the right issues, either. If I'm dealing with the fact that my brother got caught with a small amount of marijuana and is now facing a long, mandatory prison sentence, why are you talking to me about Social Security? If I'm about to lose my brother for twenty years, I don't want to hear about your tax cut! Or something that's gonna help me thirty years from now. I need to hear about right now, today. I can't even imagine living another thirty years!

I believe most black people have given it up to God anyway. Whether young or old, we just don't have the patience to wait on the political process anymore. God is the only one who has the power to deliver us, so we'll wait for Him to make a change—and maybe put a true revolutionary in office.

Don't get me wrong. Young people absolutely respect the freedom, opportunities, and blessings that we have as Americans. I know, personally, that I wouldn't have been able to achieve half as much as I have in my life and career if it wasn't for being an American. But when it comes to politics, what our country is about doesn't feel truthfully represented. I just feel like I'm being manipulated all the time.

What it should be about is honesty and passion. Young people love what is true and real. That's why we need some fistfights to go down in the Senate. Someone needs to have the kind of energy that makes them wanna lock the doors and force agreement on an issue because they believe in it so much. That's the vibe leaders like Al Sharpton and Louis Farrakhan have. Even Ted

Kennedy. Those three are the closest thing we have to political revolutionaries nowadays. They're not scared. They're willing to turn up the heat and make some noise. They're willing to stand up for what they believe in.

Bill Clinton was the only national politician we've had recently who came close to being real like that. That's why it was no surprise to me that he got so many young people to step out and vote for him. He was so heavily criticized for going on MTV, but that was one of the smartest moves he made in his campaign. Clinton knew that just showing up on a few college campuses to talk about financial aid wasn't enough; he needed to take his message to as many young people as possible. What better vehicle than MTV? And yeah, the kids asked him whether he wore boxers or briefs, but he had a cool comeback and that moment really stuck in the minds of his young voters. (No surprise that the media didn't get the impact of that appearance. All they wanted to debate was whether it was "presidential" for a candidate to discuss his underwear preference on national television. Clearly, the media doesn't get young people either.)

Another good political example would be Ralph Nader. He became the goat of the 2000 election when Democrats needed an excuse for why Al Gore got the presidency stolen from him, but at least Nader was a politician who was unafraid to say what he believed in. That's why he had socially conscious artists like the Beastie Boys supporting him. He was about to shake things up and that's exactly what the game needs right now. If somehow you could market that kind of truth and conviction, market that fearless desire to change the system, young voters would follow in droves.

Democrats just need to be Democrats again. They need to represent the voices of the people they claim to represent. Instead, every day, Democrats just seem to look and act more and more like Republicans. That's not going to work. When you're running against a true Republican, you'll never out-Republican him no matter how much you soften your point of view or bring your ideas to the middle. It's time for us to get rid of all these dinner parties and no-action fund-raisers and get back to talking to the people. If you want to mobilize young people, *take an honest and meaningful message back to the streets*. That's where all the young people are. And that's how you'll win in 2004 and beyond.

Peace and God bless.

America at a Crossroads: What Democrats Need to Do to Lead America into the Future

Andrew Cuomo

ANDREW CUOMO *is a New York native. An attorney, at twenty-eight he founded Housing Enterprise for Less Privileged (HELP), which became the nation's largest private provider of transitional housing for the homeless. He practiced law as an assistant district attorney in Manhattan and served as campaign manager for his father, Mario M. Cuomo, in his successful 1982 race for governor of New York. At thirty-nine Cuomo was named Secretary of Housing and Urban Development in the Clinton administration and won awards from Harvard for his innovation and success at passing major legislation. He was a candidate for governor of New York in 2002.*

Democrats Lost in Time

FIFTEEN YEARS AGO, THERE WASN'T A SINGLE PRIVATE WEBSITE on the planet. "Internet" was barely a word. The oldest baby boomer was forty-four. Forty million American homes had no cable television. Democrats ran the House and Senate. Russia was a republic, not a country. America was aiding Iraq. Japan was our greatest economic threat. The Taliban and al Qaeda were unknown. Nuclear warfare launched by a relatively predictable communist foe posed the only security threat to America. Our borders were relatively open. The French spent francs, the Italians spent lire, and the Germans spent deutsche marks. The two things that have remained the same since 1989 is that George Bush is president and we have the largest budget deficit in history.

It is a fact of politics that the party that best understands the forces of change and can see to the next horizon most clearly becomes the dominant political party. Democrats lost elections in 2000 and 2002 because we were lost in time. We showed little understanding of the vast changes in the world and were unresponsive to the needs of the times. We expressed no clear vision for the future. We had become the party of fear instead of the party of hope—spending more time warning what Republicans would take away rather than we did on what Democrats had to offer. To voters, we seemed bloodless, soulless, and clueless. It is not because we are a party devoid of ideas, passion, or soul but because we fooled ourselves into a political strategy of timidity. In the most recent election, Democrats feared appearing in stark contrast to a popular president and thereby failed to offer a competing vision of the future. Al From and Bruce Reed make the point succinctly: "To win the argument you must make one."

We deluded and diluted ourselves by continuing to rely on a shrinking "base vote" of Democratic voters—women, labor, minorities—who vote Democratic just enough to give the party a veneer of competitiveness but are no longer loyal or numerous enough to assure victory. The narrow margins of House and Senate Republican majorities convinced Democrats that instead of offering a bold agenda that confronted the huge issues of the day, a surgical agenda that addressed the concerns of a small number of critical demographic voters would lead us to a majority. We were overly reliant on public opinion polls that catch snapshots of voter disaffections with certain specific issues but miss the broad mosaic of the times and the mood of the country. And we fumbled the seminal moment of our lives—the terrorist attacks of 9/11.

One can argue against the logic of the Bush administration's assertion of an Iraqi connection to the 9/11 attacks or the U.S. handling of the U.N. resolution, but the Republican response to 9/11 was politically effective. The president exemplified leadership at a time when America was desperate for a leader. He deserves credit, as do congressional Republicans, for recognizing the challenge of 9/11 and rising to it.

Meanwhile, on the Democratic side there was chaos. There was no clear Democratic position on important issues of the moment—again, not because the party was devoid of good ideas, but because we handled 9/11 like it was a debate over a highway bill instead of a matter of people's lives. For example, the Department of Homeland Security was a Democratic idea (authored by Connecticut Senator Joe Lieberman) that was originally opposed by the president. But in the end, it was Republicans who tarred Democrats for tying up the Homeland Security bill over special-interest labor amendments. It was a total misreading of the times and the mood of the country, and it cost two Democratic incumbents their seats in the Senate (Max Cleland of Georgia and Jean Carnahan of Missouri) and thereby cost Democrats control of the Senate. It also left an indelible impression of Democrats choosing special interests over the security interests of the nation.

In Iraq, the Democratic Party was neither a clear critic nor a proponent of the president. We did not effectively question the president's evidence and logic nor his long-term plan for nation-building at the conclusion of the military effort. Neither did we lead the charge. Mostly, we were decidedly ambivalent.

Because Democrats so badly misjudged their response to 9/11, the second issue of the moment—the economic drop—did not matter. Though the Republicans struggled to camouflage the economic decline as a consequence of 9/11, the Democrats did not clearly articulate anything resembling a clear economic blueprint. This despite the fact that the Democrats had the Clinton-Gore legacy of the strongest economy in history.

Democrats, of course, lost the 2002 elections and forfeited their slim majority in the Senate. Rosy-scenario Democrats can argue that a few thousand votes here and a few thousand votes there would have kept Democrats in the majority. I think that outlook is deceptive and not constructive. We managed to keep a few races close mostly because of our base of minority voters, nine out of ten of whom still vote for Democrats. For example, in the Georgia governor's race, the Democratic incumbent, NRA-endorsed Caucasian Roy Barnes managed to win less than 20 percent of the white male vote.

Nor was our 2002 loss isolated. We also lost a bigger election we should have easily won: the 2000 Gore-Bush election.

My point is that denial is dangerous: acknowledge the loss, learn from it, and move forward.

Finding Our Way

John F. Kennedy said that success has many fathers, but failure is an orphan. In the Democratic Party, however, failure resembles a circular firing squad. The debate raging in the Democratic Party is whether to move ideologically to the left to appeal to our liberal base voters or to the Clintonian center where the crucial swing voters live. Presidential hopeful Howard Dean of Vermont, easily the most liberal candidate in the race not named Sharpton, brought a partisan crowd to its feet by proclaiming that he represented the Democratic wing of the Democratic Party—a reference to his clear liberal philosophy.

Other Democrats claim the problem is exactly the opposite. The centrist wing of the Democratic Party blames election failures on a shift too far to the left of the political spectrum, pointing to landslide losses by liberal icons McGovern, Mondale, and Dukakis. And Kennedy School of Government student Tim Ashe is largely right when he says that "any observer with an ear to the ground can agree that most people (including many members of Congress) want to be called a liberal like they want to drink poison."

I believe the left-right debate misses the mark and is a trap for the Democratic Party. The question is not left or right, but forward or backward.

For the Democrats to become a national force again we must prove that we have what it takes. I believe we must take several essential steps in order to do so.

We must reconnect with our soul, rediscovering the principles that made the Democratic Party the leader of every progressive movement of the twentieth century. We need to have the courage of conviction and contrast Democratic principles with Republican Party principles, making those differences clear to American voters. We have to be honest and acknowledge that many programs championed by the party are now stale and obsolete. And we must have the vision and courage to chart a concrete, forward-looking agenda consistent with our ideals.

It's Our Principles, Stupid

The Democratic agenda has gone through a process of "moderation," "reinvention," and "triangulation." But the core Democratic principles are fundamentally different from Republican principles. That is why the first step for Democrats is to step back and rediscover our soul: reacquaint ourselves with what made the Democratic Party the nation's progressive force. I am a Democrat not because I prefer a donkey to an elephant as a lapel pin, but because the Democratic Party has proven to be the vehicle for the most progressive and positive changes for this nation.

Historically, the Democratic Party has been responsible for our greatest national advancements, and a common philosophical framework drove these initiatives. These are the principles that allowed Franklin Roosevelt to create Social Security in the 1930s and that led the major progressive movements in this nation's history—civil rights, women's rights, the New Deal, the Fair Deal, the Marshall Plan, the war on poverty, disability rights, and the race to the moon. These are the same principles that gave us the Truman Doctrine and the containment of communism. These aren't liberal, centrist, or conservative principles—but Democratic principles.

True Democrats are aggressive progressives. We challenge the status quo, norms, and biases. For Democrats, the ideal society is a purely just and compassionate society. Therefore, Democratic success means a country where no child sleeps in poverty, where there are no victims of discrimination, where everyone has clean, decent, and affordable housing, where each child receives a high-quality public education, where there is a safety net for people who require assistance, and where the United States is a respected beacon of democracy and freedom for every country on the globe. Of course, this is an idealistic and optimistic worldview. Therefore, the Democratic agenda is a call to arms. It is an ongoing struggle; it is a journey more than a destination. I will accept the criticism that we are too optimistic, ambitious, and hopeful for America's potential and future. We are indeed optimists, constantly raising the bar and believing in an America that can be better than it is.

To me, the essence of the Democratic philosophy is the concept of "justice" in its fullest sense: social justice, economic justice, and racial justice.

Our crusade for social justice is based on the concept of "community." Community is derived from the Latin *communitas*—

of the common. We promote individual growth but also believe in the collective good. We believe that each individual is vested in the success or failure of each other individual, so we seek to promote success for all by providing the means to maximize opportunity. Because social justice dictates a sense of compassion and caring, we weave a safety net to protect those who cannot help themselves. We believe, as Hubert Humphrey said, that "the moral test of government is how that government treats those who are in the dawn of life, the children; those who are in the twilight of life, the elderly; and those who are in the shadows of life, the sick, the needy, and the handicapped."

We believe in racial justice. We believe it is un-American and repugnant to allow a person to be judged by race, color, or for that matter, creed, gender, or orientation. As Martin Luther King wrote from his Birmingham prison cell that "injustice anywhere is a threat to justice everywhere," Democrats believed we were duty bound to lead this country out of the shadows of discrimination and into the sunlight of equality. "We speak for the minorities who have not yet entered the mainstream. We speak for ethnics who want to add their culture to the magnificent mosaic that is America," as my father, Mario Cuomo, said at the Democratic National Convention in 1984. We believe that diversity is a strength and not a weakness, and that is why we open our arms to new legal immigrants as an infusion of talent to our great democracy.

We believe in economic justice. We believe that anyone who works full-time should live above poverty. We believe labor unions protect fairness at the negotiation tables. Because we believe that a rising tide must lift all boats, we believe in a tax system that creates opportunities for working people and promotes economic growth; we oppose a system that is stacked in favor of the privileged few who have the wherewithal and access to put their narrow interests above the public's interest.

It's our principles, stupid—to paraphrase the slogan was posted on the wall of the 1992 Clinton campaign "war room." Republican strategist Frank Luntz succinctly writes that in previous elections "Democrats lost their voice." He is right. We have to rediscover our principles and make them the basis of an aggressive progressive movement that fights for justice for all in the broadest sense.

Articulate the Differences

Democrats must not be afraid to be Democrats, to lead with our principles, not (as is our habit) with programs. We must also be eager to draw the distinction between Democratic and Republican principles.

Republicans have a clear credo. They promise free-market economics, less government, lower taxes, strong defense, local control, and individual liberty. Republicans are more accepting of the free-market economy and its results. They want to rely totally on our system of capitalism to render just consequences. They believe that the wealthy are the engines of our economy and that a tax system that benefits the most affluent will have long-term benefits for the middle and lower classes. Republicans fear government will hold back America's potential. They believe that left to its own devices, business can be trusted to make the right decisions for the public—*the business of America is business* and *what's good for General Motors is good for America.*

Democrats question the results of our economy as sometimes unjust or unproductive and in need of correction. We question the concentration of economic power and see government as a necessary check on the system to ensure fair treatment for all people. Democrats see government as a means to fulfill each individual's potential by leveling the playing field, removing obstacles, and striving to provide opportunity for all.

Instead of blurring the distinctions in vision that separate the two parties, Democrats should sharpen and underscore them. Harry Truman understood: "[Republicans] have a hard time hearing what the ordinary people of the country are saying . . . [But] they are able to catch the slightest whisper from big business and the special interests." That contrast is a lot sharper than the Democratic line today, when trying to pare a $750 billion GOP tax cut to a $350 billion GOP-lite tax cut. Harry Truman won his election. We lost ours.

Old Principles: New Solutions

For the Democratic Party, the truth is that while our principles remain fresh, some of our solutions have become stale—disillusioning people who want results, not just rhetoric.

Our operating premise is that government can play a role in improving society. Therefore the burden is on the Democrats to design and manage a government that can do that. The Republicans win the debate when the government fails. Waste, fraud, and abuse are the three favorite words of the Republicans. Their argument is that of impossibility. They seldom challenge our goals of, for example, affordable housing, job training, and economic development; rather, the Republicans challenge the means to these goals, the failed government programs that doom the Democrats' efforts.

A progressive movement by definition undertakes difficult tasks, and therefore we must always be willing to experiment with new solutions and to disregard failed attempts before they become poster children for waste. Democrats should not have waited until the Gingrich revolution in 1994 to reform welfare. We ignored the data that showed that for many families, welfare was a trap that kept them in poverty. We should not have waited thirty years to reform public housing in order to construct healthy integrated communities instead of ghettos that warehoused the poor.

We became wedded to our programs and lost the principles that they were meant to implement. We must be willing to admit error, confront obsolescence, and throw out the old, tired ideas. We are only as good as our best ideas.

Charting the Course

The final step Democrats need to take is to translate our philosophical core into a road map for the nation's future. We must apply our principles to the changing times and develop an agenda to carry America forward. We need both a macro vision and a road map to implement that vision. New York State is a microcosm of the United States. We have large urban tracts and some of the most sparse rural areas in the country. Farming is one of the largest industries in the state, as is manufacturing. And members of every ethnic and racial group call New York home. As a candidate for governor in New York State, I identified many issues that I believed posed a threat to our commonly held values and required immediate attention from our leaders in state government. The national debate has pointed to additional challenges. Here I focus on the lessons learned in New York that apply to the entire nation.

1. Security

The most pressing challenge for this nation is homeland defense. Despite many important steps forward, neither party has yet outlined a complete agenda that both tackles this enormous task and ensures that we do not abandon our most treasured civil liberties and institutions in the process.

As a general rule, Republicans tend to overestimate national security threats and Democrats underestimate them. This is a time when most Americans would rather be safe than sorry and are more receptive to Republicans. Because Republicans have mostly been in charge at all levels of government post–9/11, the Republican response has been a blizzard of activity, not all of it helpful: the creation of a new Washington bureaucracy, daily alerts utilizing colors of the rainbow, and dubious new federal powers to detain and interrogate Americans and others indefinitely without indictment or counsel. Since September 11, Democrats have made important points concerning port defense and other isolated priorities but have failed to approach the problem with the urgency or comprehensiveness that it demands. Nor have there been any real efforts to debate the toll taken on our values and our rights as a society by the new federal detention powers.

There is a tremendous void to fill where systems should be in place to keep America as safe as possible and minimize casualties if a terrorist strike occurs. Nearly two years after 9/11, 97 percent of the cargo that comes through the nation's ports goes uninspected. Most local jurisdictions still lack the capacity to integrate communications and functions of the three major emergency personnel first on the scene of a terrorist attack: police, firefighters, and medical workers. The National Guard in most states does not have sufficient personnel to deal with a large-scale terrorist attack because too many guardsmen are also local police or firefighters. Adequate airport perimeter security, particularly for smaller airfields, remains beyond the budget capacity of many facilities across the country. And the public health infrastructure necessary to ensure immediate recognition and containment of bioterrorism remains the victim of underinvestment. We must have a comprehensive plan funded by the federal government that fundamentally upgrades our approach to public safety at virtually every level of society and in every public space. States cannot do it alone, nor should they have to try. Democrats can and should be the party that ensures our safety through comprehensive planning and federal investments.

2. Providing Economic Justice and Opportunity

Leadership requires policies that both improve the national and local economies and, at the same time, ensure that all Americans have the opportunity to share in the prosperity we create. In New York State, despite a prolonged period of economic growth during the late 1990s, the gap between the wealthy and the poor increased dramatically. The same trend has occurred across the country. Despite this disturbing threat to our nation's cohesion and to our values of economic justice for all hardworking Americans, Republicans continue to seek improvident tax cuts for the wealthiest Americans at the expense of both middle-class Americans and the ideal of fiscal discipline. As Peter Peterson notes in his insightful essay, the Republican obsession with tax cuts at any cost has succeeded in turning a surplus into a deficit.

Democratic values dictate a greater sensitivity to the impact of tax cuts on less-wealthy Americans and a greater concern for the economic implications of expanding the nation's deficit, as the Reagan administration did in the 1980s. At a time when states face enormous security costs and a host of federal mandates, the Republican tax cut agenda for the wealthy inevitably spells cuts to critical state and local services and schools, which we cannot afford. Accordingly, this latest Republican threat to our common values—values shared by most Americans—must be met with a commitment to fiscal discipline and increased financial support for the states. Democrats must lead the fight to eliminate our deficit to spur the national economy and use precious federal resources to support state spending on basic services and education for all.

How can Democrats be both fiscally responsible and improve services? As a candidate for governor, I proposed a consolidation tax-credit program to increase the efficiency of government, lower taxes, and improve services. It worked like this: local governmental jurisdictions (like adjoining counties, for example) that consolidate services or operations would receive two benefits from the state above and beyond the obvious savings from higher efficiency. First, the state would provide a tax rebate to taxpaying residents of the jurisdiction(s) worth 10 percent of the projected savings from consolidation. Second, the local governments themselves would receive a "consolidation incentive bonus" to support local government functions. Together, these incentives would motivate residents to pressure their local elected officials to pursue consolidation in order to obtain much-needed tax relief. Over time the program would increase efficiency and reduce local tax burdens at a substantial discount to the state government. Democrats must find creative ways to stretch scarce revenues to promote economic growth for everyone.

3. Educating Our Children

Democrats' belief in social, economic, and racial justice all require a deep commitment to offering every child a sound education. We are connected by the fabric of society and linked by a common community: the better an individual does, the better for society. We believe in mobility and diversity and government's assistance in those goals. Education must be a priority, but it is also an area where we recognize that our policy prescriptions have become so stale that our values are threatened.

Our schools have become a political battleground without any winners, but with plenty of losers: the children who suffer year after year in a poor educational system. The painful truth today is that there are two types of educational systems, not just public and private, but also rich and poor. Republicans urge privatization and vouchers, while Democrats battle for more funds for public education. Republicans stress lack of accountability while Democrats claim inadequate resources. Democrats must stick to their principles of supporting our public schools, but they also must not be afraid to embrace new solutions and increased accountability to improve them.

Vouchers for private school are not the panacea that the Republicans would have people believe, and they threaten to undermine our existing public schools. Charter schools hold selective promise, but are only a part of the answer. We must embrace comprehensive reform of our public school system that does not continually seek, as the Republicans often do, simply to remove children from, or undermine, those systems.

Research has demonstrated that dramatic improvements flow from sound reforms within the system: better training and recruitment of our teachers combined with high expectations and rewards for performance; close supervision and training for principals to lead our schools and ensure accountability; intensive literacy initiatives to train both teachers and students to ensure that every child is reading by the third grade; smaller high schools to improve the learning process and foster smaller communities; and substantial parental involvement initiatives that extend a child's learning to the home, among other reforms. In addition, we must be willing to close persistently failing schools that have not responded to help, in favor of new schools with new staff and new approaches. Democrats are the party of public education and therefore we must be the party that demands the most from public education.

We must also make the United States the leader in early education. Research tells us that 75 percent of a child's brain development occurs before the age of five, and that early education can make a profound difference in a child's future. In addition to efforts to provide pre-kindergarten more universally, pilot programs in some states have shown that learning can and should begin at age three. Several states have also launched comprehensive reforms to their child care delivery systems to provide subsidized early education as part of state-funded day care programs. Universal pre-K for four-year-olds should be realized as soon as possible across the country; but our ambitions for our children should extend beyond that to providing "Universal 3-K" for all of our three-year-olds as well. Early education is good for our children, but it's also good for our nation.

These are just some of the policies that serve the Democratic commitment to providing a sound education to every child without abandoning, as many Republicans would, the promise of public education.

4. Protecting Our Environment and Increasing Our Energy Supply

Few issues better illustrate the difference in values between Democrats and Republicans than our protection of the environment in which we live. Once again, our values are being threatened. Leading Republicans continue to take their cues from industrial polluters and oil companies rather than from the voters. The Bush administration and the congressional Republicans have initiated a far-reaching and destructive agenda to weaken key environmental safeguards. In the short period since the election, federal agencies have announced more than one hundred changes to weaken environmental protections. By changing the so-called new-source-review program, the Republicans seek to let the nation's oldest and dirtiest power plants and refineries expand and modernize without installing updated pollution controls. The Bush administration seeks to eliminate the requirement that forest-management plans protect wildlife. In early January 2003, the EPA announced plans for new policies to reduce the number of wetlands and waterways protected by the Clean Water Act. These are just a few of the assaults on our environment that Republicans have mounted.

Sprawling land development is consuming the American countryside at a rate of almost 365 acres per hour. Traffic and pollution combine with this loss of pristine landscapes to undermine our quality of life, our productivity, and our public health. Democrats understand that it is time to make a U-turn on the development highway and focus once again on developing our cities and our existing suburbs with a more sustainable long-term approach. That means restoring our abandoned industrial sites to productive uses, encouraging inner-city development rather than subsidizing sprawl, and developing balancing development with preservation.

While Republicans continue their efforts to drill for oil in the pristine Alaskan Wildlife Refuge, Democrats understand that the amount of oil we could obtain through such drilling pales in comparison with the nearly two billion barrels we could save every day simply from raising fuel-economy standards. That is more oil than we imported from Saudi Arabia in 2002, and three times our imports from Iraq. Democrats understand that renewable energy and true support for hybrid vehicles can make the difference between our nation's costly dependence on foreign oil and a cleaner, more independent future.

The key challenge facing particularly the largest states in their quest to be economically competitive is that of ensuring sufficient supplies of inexpensive energy for commercial, industrial, and residential uses. California's recent crisis showed the pitfalls of relying exclusively on deregulation to guarantee a market for energy. New York's efforts to deregulate have produced the worst of both worlds: the high prices of a regulated market combined with the uncertainty of a free market. In addition, a deep credit crunch after the Enron debacle has brought new energy investments to a standstill.

In addition, the pollution from power generators—including sulfur dioxide and nitrogen oxide—has been shown to cause lung cancer, asthma, and acute bronchitis. Children are particularly vulnerable to asthma. These air pollutants also are responsible for the acid rain that continues to destroy the lakes and streams of the Northeast. Nearly one in four lakes in New York State's Adirondacks are so acidic that they can no longer sustain fish life.

Greenhouse gas emissions—principally carbon dioxide— have also accelerated a global warming trend that threatens our agricultural and tourism industries and produces harmful health effects. Without efforts to reduce greenhouse gas emissions, total emissions in New York State alone are expected to be 12 percent higher in 2010 than in 1990, compared to the Kyoto Protocol targets of 7 percent below 1990 levels.

The solution to this crisis, again, requires new solutions that transcend the old debate between deregulation and state control, economic growth and environmental protection. The truth is that technology has provided several ways to increase our energy supply dramatically while preserving our environment. In New York State, for example, many older power plants remain in operation despite their inefficiency and resultant polluting. A process known as "repowering" is available to retrofit these plants with new technologies that boost power production while cutting emissions dramatically. Unfortunately, neither states nor the federal government have provided support for repowering by private-sector energy companies during this credit crunch. Instead, states like New York have chosen to rely on sitting emergency generators that are stop-gap solutions and produce harmful emissions.

To address this problem, our federal and state governments should provide tax credits to existing power plants to offset the costs of repowering older, less efficient technology with newer, cleaner, more efficient technology. To be eligible, the power plants should be required to cut acid rain and ozone-causing pollutants and emissions of particulate matter, and to increase power generation substantially. Such programs would reduce airborne pollutants dramatically, improve the economy, and save consumers and businesses on their energy costs. Savings to consumers will come principally from the increased supply of energy from newer, more efficient plants that cut the costs of energy production significantly. In addition, where revamped plants are located near demand, in high-demand areas, there would be fewer losses associated with delivering power over long distances, and less congestion across the power grid.

It is time for the Democrats to provide a bold agenda for energy and environmental progress that boosts our economy and our quality of life.

5. Racial Justice

The Democratic Party believes in racial justice and therefore acknowledges the continuing racism and discrimination that exists in our country. Mostly because of Democratic efforts to try and solve America's most difficult problem, we have made tremendous progress since the '60s. Our Republican brethren, however, behave as if the work to make America a truly equal society is completed. They are in denial.

During my tenure as HUD secretary, I was responsible for enforcing antidiscrimination laws and was outraged at the continued violations and our nation's apparent complacency. The fact remains that an African American earning $60,000 is more likely to be turned down for a home loan than a white person earning $40,000. Our housing stock remains largely segregated, as do our schools. To compound this problem, our enforcement of civil rights, fair housing, and equal employment laws is lax at best. In New York, a civil rights case filed today will be heard in 2010. Justice delayed is justice denied.

The nation has not yet come to terms with black-white relations; how will it come to terms when we are a nation of thirty different races with whites in the minority? Democrats should champion racial and ethnic justice and bring a new diligence and drive in enforcing the antidiscrimination laws. We should show equal outrage at a discrimination violation as at a drug violation. We must work aggressively to end the current situation, where antidiscrimination-law violations are essentially second-class complaints.

6. Creating a More Responsive Government
for the People

Democrats at their best stand for cleaner, more responsive government that serves the interests of the voters rather than just the special interests and large corporations. Unlike most Republicans, they have embraced reforms to make those principles a reality year in and year out. Most recently, the federal battle for campaign finance legislation succeeded only because Democrats fought Republican leadership and found a sturdy ally in an iconoclastic Republican named McCain, who was willing to buck his party's line to promote real change.

But the fight is not over. Washington has returned to the culture of influence-peddling. The Bush White House has raised more money in large, six-figure donations than any administration in history. Companies like Halliburton and Enron would appear to have an office in the White House and routinely obtain lucrative contracts and have disproportionate influence over our national policy. Democrats must continue to fight for reforms to improve not only the policies of our government but also the process by which those policies are settled. On the federal level, we must pass the next generation of campaign finance reforms. For example, we need to defend and expand our campaign finance laws to provide free air time to candidates and level the playing field for democracy. In this area, it's no accident that Democrats stand for "democracy" in the truest sense. We also must eliminate the loophole in McCain-Feingold that allows people to give unlimited sums anonymously to shadow organizations that run ads for or against candidates. In the various states, we need to lead efforts to put in place reasonable public campaign financing and spending limits to open up the political process and remove the corrosive effects of massive campaign contributions. We also need to pass more stringent lobbying laws in many states, including New York, to eliminate the practice of taking campaign contributions with one hand and giving out public contracts with the other.

With these and other initiatives, Democrats must retake the mantle of reform and responsive government, and demonstrate much more powerfully the profound differences in values and solutions between the two major parties.

Build It and They Will Come

The Youth

Not since John F. Kennedy has there been a politician who has inspired a generation of young people to enter public service. The Democratic Party as the reform and progressive vehicle has always been the natural platform for young people in this country. But voting rates among those under the age of twenty-five declined from 40.7 percent in 1980 to 26.3 percent in 2000. There remains a public-spiritedness, but the young would rather volunteer in a soup kitchen than work in the local city hall. Government as a vehicle for social change has been discredited. There is no magic solution. I have visited dozens of colleges to discuss the topic and was recently at Harvard working on the problem. A progressive agenda will attract youth if it is honest and bold and is communicated to them. "The strength of the Democratic Party has rested with its ability to challenge the status quo and offer

Americans, especially young Americans, new ideas and a purpose greater than their own," write Harvard sophomores Andrew Frank and Joel Washington.

While I was at HUD we launched a special effort to bring younger people into government and we received eight thousand applications from the nation's "best and brightest" to fill two hundred positions. Their appetite for involvement is still present if there is a specific effort to defeat their cynicism.

Senator John Kerry writes that "instead of just quoting the words of Franklin Roosevelt and John Kennedy and Robert Kennedy, we need to match their leadership with our own, with daring and commitment, with new thinking equal to a new and different time." The audience is attentive if the message is honest and right.

The Curse of the Polls

Democrats and Republicans alike have become obsessed with polls. Polls have become the operating manual of the modern-day political machines. But in many ways polls are misleading and certainly limiting. Polls can only tell you where people are today, not where they could be tomorrow if led. They don't give the American people enough credit for intelligence, judgment, and the ability to rise to the moment. Polls suggest a self-fulfilling prophecy that says the American people will respond only if they are approached on their narrow self-interest. Polls turn leaders into followers.

Politics requires a belief in the people, and political leaders must fully trust in that belief. Our politics has become too scripted, too adulterated, too orchestrated. Politicians should talk more not less: from their hearts as well as their heads. The American people can detect sincerity and honesty. If a leader is to earn our trust, he or she must be forthcoming. We sometimes forget that half truths are half lies and that candor counts. Authenticity in leadership is preferable to orchestration. People don't expect perfect leaders: they would rather have a genuine relationship. If people know where their leader is coming from—personally and ideologically—they will be more willing to have faith in where he or she wants to take them.

It is clear to me that we cannot develop a progressive Democratic agenda to move this country forward if all we do is adhere to polling prescriptions. The Reverend Al Sharpton writes how "Dr. Martin Luther King, Jr., used to describe two types of leaders: Thermometers measure the temperature and move based on the climate of the day . . . then there are thermostat leaders that change the temperature, that change the political climate to make progress more possible."

Dr. King understood that ideas that challenge the status quo and seek to solve the very difficult problems that face America can appeal to voters. We must believe that people will follow a leader they trust on a course that goes beyond their own self-interest. It may seem like a quaint notion, but that is how every great progressive movement of the past has succeeded. If we waited until polls told leaders the coast was clear, Jackie Robinson might never have been a Brooklyn Dodger, Europe would never have been rebuilt, and the Great Society would not have happened.

The Democratic agenda is never easy. A progressive approach challenges power structures and mediocrity. It appeals to our better angels when it is often easier to appeal to fear and anger. It requires the ability to take risks.

The Republican theory is in many ways less challenging. Less government, less taxes, less regulation, less United Nations has a certain appeal to it. Allowing free-market forces to determine winners and losers absolves any of us from responsibility. But that is the difference between Democrats and Republicans.

Our founding fathers showed that politics is about stark contrast, deeply held beliefs, and hard-fought campaigns. Politics must be about a passion for principles. Statesmen like Jefferson and Adams did not hide their differences but highlighted them. Politics was a difficult business, a tough fight that was in many ways more contentious than it is today. *Democrats must realize the good fight is a fight.* You can't make everyone happy. The business of government is the business of leadership.

America is at a crossroads, and it is time for leaders to lead. Historically, times like this have brought out the best in the Democratic Party and the American people.

Yes, we have challenges but we will rise to the occasion and be the better for it.

People are poised for change. This is a potential progressive moment for this nation. The Democratic Party should, once again, lead the way.

September 11 and the 2002 Midterm Elections

Governor Gray Davis

GRAY DAVIS *is the thirty-seventh governor of California and only the fourth Democrat in the last one hundred years to hold that office. His long record of public service includes four years as lieutenant governor, eight years as state comptroller, and six years as a member of the state assembly. As a captain in the United States Army he was awarded a Bronze Star for meritorious service during the Vietnam War. He earned a B.A. from Stanford University in 1964 and a J.D. from Columbia University Law School in 1967.*

LIKE ALL THINGS IN AMERICAN LIFE AT THAT TIPPING POINT IN history, the 2002 elections were reflected through a prism of post– 9/11 attitudes and anxieties.

More than a full year after we'd come face-to-face with our worst fears and our better angels, Americans had returned to normalcy—but not complacency.

Peace and prosperity and irrational exuberance were yesterday's news. Now the world's greatest and only remaining superpower was keenly aware of its own vulnerabilities.

Every time we went to the airport, every time we passed through metal detectors just to see a baseball game, every time we simply opened our mail, we were reminded that homeland security was still an objective, not an achievement.

In 2002, the threat of terror didn't run our lives, but we ran our lives around it. It wasn't always our focus, but it was still our fear.

At the same time, Americans found renewed comfort in American things—the flag, the anthem, the Pledge, pride in our community and our country.

We also found new heroes, genuine heroes—not the running back who rushed for a thousand yards or the actor whose movie grossed $100 million, but honest-to-goodness, liberty-before-life American heroes:

- The firefighters and police officers who charged headlong into the mouth of sacrifice
- The bond traders and businessmen who were last seen helping complete strangers down the stairs
- The 246 airline passengers bound for California—some

of whom summoned epic courage in a final stand against terror

- The beloved fire chaplain who died giving last rites to a fallen fireman
- The search-and-rescue teams who gave every waking hour in a valley of death to the hope of finding life
- The United States armed forces who continue to defend the cause of freedom and justice far from home, but not far from our hearts

Against this backdrop of American heroism in the face of senseless hatred, Americans united behind a common commitment to overcoming evil with good. People donated their time and their savings. Children emptied their piggy banks to help people they'd never met—in places they'd never heard of. Americans of every faith, race, and financial status came together in an offer of hope and healing.

More than at any time since World War II, we were one nation under God. We supported our troops. We supported our government. And we especially supported that unique person in our democracy in whom those things come together: our commander in chief.

In the weeks that followed 9/11, there were no partisans, only patriots. Democrats and Republicans alike stood foursquare behind the War on Terror and the defense of our land here at home.

But no measure of love for country could mask the problems still plaguing our nation: a declining economy, a struggling health care system, the slow erosion of environmental regulation, and a glaring lack of accountability within many of America's corporations. Americans all across the country were suffering—and not just because we'd been awakened to evil. In truth, the economy was faltering long before 9/11. Exports were down. Markets were in free fall. Jobs were being lost. President Bush was set to take a hit. But 9/11 hit first.

As tragedy in 2001 became resiliency in 2002, Democratic officeholders and candidates became more and more emboldened and began pointing to our national problems. In turn, the American public became more and more aware of these problems and began demanding action.

But the popular wartime president, widely seen as the global guardian of freedom from the forces of fear, was able to stay high above the fray. Unlike with the 1992 elections after the Gulf War, the international threat that united our countrymen and -women was ongoing. As long as fear was still a factor, the American public wanted to know that their president was hard at work, defending their security, while they worked, played, and dreamed.

In this environment, anything wrong with America was cast as the product of evildoing. And, like no others before him, this president successfully presented his administration and its allies as evildoing's worst enemy. The economy and other problems were swept under the president's security blanket. When he wasn't seen defending our homeland, President Bush could be found out campaigning for Republican candidates.

In fact, no president in modern American history has ever devoted more time to actively campaigning for other candidates. Predictably, each race became an individual referendum on the president's agenda. The 2002 election stripped down to its bare essentials, then, featured a false choice: between the president's good security/bad economy and the opposition's bad security/ good economy.

"Economically insecure but physically safe" won in a landslide. That isn't to say that the party in power avoided the blame for our national ills. Voter outrage simply trickled down from the White House to the statehouse. And governors, perhaps more than any other elected officials, bore the heavy weight of a national economy that went from boom to a very loud thud.

In 2002, there were open races for governor in twenty-one states. The party in power lost seventeen. Traditionally, incumbency is a huge advantage. And yet, of the five Democratic governors running for reelection, only two survived: Governor Tom Vilsack of Iowa and myself. Believe me, I count myself as extremely fortunate to have squeaked by with a five-point victory. Across America, voters seemed to agree on two things: that it's a governor's responsibility to mind the store while the president is preoccupied with terror, and that their own governor was not doing a very good job of it.

But our fifty states represent the front line in the fight for homeland security. Our police officers, our firefighters, and our rescue workers are the finest first-responder force the world has ever known. Our National Guard has stood watch over our airports and vital systems. Our hospitals and health care workers continue to prepare for the threat of bioterrorism. And state governments are footing the bill. Washington might serve as a center of operations for homeland security, but the states are where the rubber hits the road.

Nevertheless, these are still *international* affairs. And, fair or not, governors receive little of the credit for protecting our people from terror and most of the blame for America's remaining domestic challenges. With 2004 around the corner, this shift of responsibilities doesn't appear to be easing.

While the federal Treasury continues to print money and the federal budget bleeds red, governors must balance their budgets while doing far more with less. They must strengthen education and health care. They must protect the safety of their people. They must stimulate the economy and create new jobs.

By any measure, it's both a difficult load and a delicate balancing act. But it is also the latest test of gubernatorial leadership, as evidenced by the 2002 elections.

Taking Our Country Back:
A Democratic Vision for America

Governor Howard Dean, M.D.

HOWARD DEAN was elected governor of Vermont in 1991 after serving in the Vermont House from 1982 to 1986 and as lieutenant governor in 1986. He is a physician who previously shared a medical practice with his wife, Dr. Judith Steinberg. Governor Dean is currently working hard on his Democratic presidential campaign, continuing his lifelong mission of securing a brighter future for our kids.

THE REPUBLICAN VICTORY IN THE 2002 ELECTION, WHILE LARGE enough to give them control of Congress, was still a narrow one. A switch in the right races of a mere 0.1 percent of the national vote would have put Democrats in control of both the Senate and the House. Americans remain almost exactly divided between the two parties, and there is no indication that the Republican victory last year signals any lasting national political shift. Still, the election must teach Democrats a lesson that it is imperative that we never forget.

One factor tipping the election to the Republicans was the unnecessary weight of two key miscalculations by Democrats. First, apparently hoping to reduce the impact of national security issues, some Democrats supported legislation giving the president open-ended authority for a war with Iraq, without first requiring either that the case be made that war is necessary or that the United States attempt to work through the United Nations, the organization created precisely for such a situation. Second, even though the Democratic strategy was to focus voters on the economy, the Democrats did not stand up clearly enough against President Bush's failed economic policy of tax cut after tax cut, and did not advance a clear, positive Democratic agenda on the economy. So, on both foreign policy and the economy, the 2002 election was not a referendum on Democratic versus Republican ideals. Left without a clear choice, voters, by a slight margin, opted for Republican over Republican Lite.

This was the second straight national election that did not hinge on a difference over ideas. President Bush was able to squeak into office only by promising to be a different kind of Republican—a compassionate conservative who would change the tone in Washington, governing from a bipartisan consensus. He will not be able to run the same way for reelection, as he has not governed as he promised. Instead, he is now revealed as an unrepentant conservative, subscribing to the dangerously narrow orthodoxy of today's national Republican leadership.

So the stage is set for an honest debate in 2004 on the real differences between Democrats and Republicans. President Bush has a record that reveals his true colors. Democrats are now energized to stand up for our core beliefs.

I am optimistic that, with Democrats forthrightly presenting our values and our vision, the voters will side with us—perhaps conclusively enough to make the next election one that ushers in a lasting transformation of American politics. My optimism is rooted in confidence that the core beliefs of the Democratic Party are particularly well aligned with the emerging values and changing demographics of the United States in the twenty-first century.

The difference between the parties begins here: today's Republicans favor the few. On economic matters, they favor the fortunate few who already have it made. On social policy, they favor the extremist few on the far right, whose views they try to impose on the rest of us.

Democrats value all Americans. We do so because we appreciate the individual worth of all Americans, regardless of their background or persuasion. We also know that whenever any American can participate in and contribute to our nation to the full extent of his or her own ability, we all benefit. We offer, to every individual, every family, and every community, opportunity and hope, and we expect, in turn, responsibility.

These values lead to policies that match well what today's Americans want, need, and deserve.

Democrats are committed to making available decent health care to all Americans. No child should miss a regular checkup because her parents cannot afford the doctor's fee, and no grand-parent should have to choose between medication and food. No worker should be a layoff away from losing health insurance, and no family should be a major illness away from bankruptcy. We Democrats will—soon—complete the mission of Harry Truman, John F. Kennedy, Lyndon Johnson, Jimmy Carter, and Bill Clinton by making adequate, affordable health insurance available to all children and all adults.

Democrats champion equal opportunities and equal rights for all Americans, regardless of background, economic standing, race, gender, or sexual orientation. We are committed to having a government that really looks like America, so that it can truly represent, connect with, and stand up for the real America. Knowing that education opens doors for all Americans, we promote excellence in public education and resist diverting taxpayer money to private schools open to only a few. We oppose excessive government interference in matters of personal privacy, from reproductive freedom to religious freedom.

Democrats know that social progress depends on prudent management of our money. Just as responsible parents are concerned about saving for their children's education, we are dedicated to seeing that the next generation has the opportunity to meet their needs. As Democrats have done in the past, we will exercise the fiscal discipline to live within our means, balance our budgets, pay down our debt, and set aside enough money for Social Security and health care for those who will soon retire.

Democrats understand that America's strength depends not only on having all the military force necessary to protect us and on the willingness to use that force when appropriate, but also on the moral force of the values that hold us together as a nation and unite us with our allies. We know that the Marshall Plan did as much for America's national security and international leadership as do any martial plans. We know that to preserve, strengthen, and use effectively our position of preeminence in the world, we need to exercise principled, responsible, and respectable leadership.

These values are more important than ever as a changing United States enters the twenty-first century. Today's Americans are increasingly diverse, in attitudes and needs as well as in racial and ethnic backgrounds. Only a government that values all Americans can shape the conditions in which all can reach their full potential. And only if all Americans can get ahead can we fulfill our national promise and achieve our full national power.

That path, paved with Democratic ideals, is the way to a stronger future. It is the course the American people are likely to choose, for 2004 and beyond.

Election Results, Rally Effects, and Democratic Futures

Professor John J. DiIulio, Jr.

JOHN J. DIIULIO, JR., is the Fox Leadership Professor at the University of Pennsylvania. With James Q. Wilson, he is the coauthor of American Government: Institutions and Policies *(Houghton Mifflin, 2003). During his academic leave in 2001, he served as assistant to the president of the United States and as first director of the White House Office of Faith-Based and Community Initiatives.*

MANY POLITICAL OBSERVERS BELIEVE THAT REPUBLICANS ENJOY major electoral advantages over Democrats. Given the president's post–9/11 popularity and the huge role that the White House reportedly played in the 2002 midterm congressional elections,[1] some predict that a pro-GOP partisan realignment could occur as early as 2004, ushered in by a Bush-led Republican sweep that would make President Reagan's 1984 reelection landslide seem small by comparison.

In contemporary American politics, almost anything is possible. The relevant empirical evidence, however, paints a more complicated picture: Republicans are not yet dominant, but neither are Democrats at all poised to regain power.

Interpreting Elections

Nearly everything we hear in the immediate aftermath of an election about what the results mean proves, upon closer inspection, to be largely or totally false. For example, in 1992, after twelve straight years in which conservative Republicans called the White House home, many morning-after analysts asserted that Americans were suddenly open to progressive policy ideas. Two years later, the same consultants and commentators confidently proclaimed that the Republican "earthquake" victory in the midterm congressional elections reflected the rise of a new and powerful bloc of voters—"angry white males." Following the 1996 Clinton reelection, there was much media hype about Democratic "soccer moms"—married suburban white women with children.[2]

---

[1] Jim VandeHei and Dan Balz, "In GOP Win, a Lesson in Money, Muscle, Planning," *The Washington Post*, November 10, 2002, A01; Howard Fineman, "How Bush Did It," *Newsweek*, November 18, 2002, 29–34, 35–37.

[2] Parts of this section are adapted from my essay "Mandate Mongering," *The Weekly Standard*, November 18, 2002, 18–20.

But as the Clinton administration learned during its first two years, most especially through the failure of its big-government health plan, in 1992 there was no emerging progressive majority. Likewise, in 1994, what felt like an electoral earthquake was really only small seismic shifts: Republicans gained fifty-four seats, but if fewer than a grand total of twenty thousand votes in just thirteen House districts had voted Democratic instead of Republican, Democrats and Tom Foley, not Republicans and Newt Gingrich, would have led the 104th Congress.

In every election from 1968 to 1992, the percentage of the popular vote for Republican candidates to the House was higher than the percentage of House seats that actually went to Republicans. For instance, in 1976 the Republicans won 42.1 percent of the vote but received only 32.9 percent of the seats. The gap is accounted for in part by the fact that Democrats tend to do very well in low-turnout districts such as minority-dominated inner cities, while Republicans tend to do better in suburban districts.

By 1992, for the first time, a majority of all House districts had suburban-majority populations. In 1994, the GOP vote-seat gap finally closed. Though only 19 percent of eligible voters cast a vote for a Republican, it was enough to best the Democrats, who won the votes of only 16.6 percent of eligible voters. Apparently, by 1996, the mythical Republican males had married the media-manufactured Democratic moms: married suburban white women with children supported Clinton over Dole, but they did so by almost exactly the same proportion as did the general electorate (49 to 42 percent); furthermore, they strongly favored congressional Republicans (55 to 45 percent).

Election myths can become gospel truths even among ostensibly data-savvy party gurus. Take, for example, the GOP orthodoxy that President George H. W. Bush lost to Clinton because he lost Republican voters by being too moderate (breaking his no-new-taxes pledge, failing to court religious conservatives, and so on). Actually, Bush 41's biggest losses were among independents and Democrats: after winning 55 percent of independents in 1988, he won only 32 percent of them in 1992; and having won 17 percent of Democrats in 1988, he won just 10 percent in 1992. Survey data suggest that, if anything, they defected because they perceived him as too far to the right on many issues.

Likewise, take the 2000 presidential election, the razor-close results of which supposedly revealed the country to be evenly divided into geographically concentrated red-Republican and blue-Democratic electoral zones. Nice and tidy maps, but there are many Democratic state and local leaders in the red zones, many Republican ones in the blue zones, and many states that voted Democratic or Republican in the 2000 national races that voted the other way twice or more since 1980. What *was* truly novel about the 2000 election results was *not* that the country was so evenly divided in popular vote terms, but that it was so evenly divided in terms of the electoral college.

The country has normally been *very* closely divided in presidential politics, and divided in ways that bunch partisan blocs by region (for example, the once Democratic but now largely Republican South). In 1980, Reagan won just 51 percent of the popular vote but 91 percent of the electoral college (EC) vote. Reagan thereby joined Truman (1948), Kennedy (1960), Nixon (1968), and Carter as a first-term president who won barely 50 percent of the popular vote. Clinton was twice a plurality-vote president. Bush 43's victory was exceptional only in that, rather than carrying 55 to 70 percent of the EC vote, he lost the popular vote and won the EC, *both* by razor-thin margins.

The 2002 midterm election results do represent a historic GOP win: "Not since 1934 has a president's party gained seats in both houses of Congress in a first-term midterm election, and not since 1882 has a midterm election transformed a divided party government into a unified one."[3]

But the GOP's 2002 victory was neither dramatic nor improbable. Republicans closed the aforementioned vote-seat gap in 1994, and have since had nearly a decade to exploit the considerable electoral advantages that, as numerous political science studies suggest, are afforded by incumbency. Since 1962, more than nine in ten House incumbents who ran for reelection won; only once since 1962 has the incumbent House party lost (1994). Likewise, in 2002, Republicans won the two closest Senate races, but a shift of just 12,000 votes in one (Missouri) and 9,500 in the other (New Hampshire) and the Democrats would have won.

Rally Effects

Still, the fact remains that Republicans now normally best Democrats at winning the close ones, and for reasons that are widely attributed to their fielding, funding, and focusing candidates (both incumbents and challengers) better, on average, than Democrats do. As one magazine phrased it, in 2002 "Bush was the driv-

[3] Marc J. Hetherington and Michael Nelson, "Anatomy of a Rally Effect: George W. Bush and the War on Terrorism," *PS: Political Science and Politics* 36:1 (January 2003): 42.

ing force behind the Republican breeze that blew across the country."[4] How likely is it that in 2004 the "breeze" will become a whirlwind?

It is, of course, impossible to predict at this stage whether the president will be reelected, and if so, by how much, or with what, if any, partisan coattails. But this much is already known: while "Bush's personal popularity affected the voting for Republican congressional candidates," the president's post–9/11 popularity has not had any impact to date on party identification.[5] Following the terrorist attacks, "Republican identification actually held steady at 32 percent" and was still "in the low 30s by June 2002."[6]

Bush's approval rating soared from 51 percent on September 10, 2001, to 86 percent on September 15, 2001, and peaked at 90 percent on September 22, 2001, the highest presidential approval rating ever recorded. This was a classic "rally effect," defined as a "sudden and substantial increase in public approval . . . that occurs in response to certain kinds of dramatic international events involving the United States."[7] By "recruiting challengers to Democratic incumbents, raising funds ardently, and campaigning tirelessly," in 2002 Bush's post–9/11 popularity helped Republican congressional candidates.[8]

---

[4] Fineman, "How Bush Did It," 36.
[5] Hetherington and Nelson, "Anatomy of a Rally Effect," 40, 42.
[6] Ibid., 40.
[7] Ibid., 37.
[8] Ibid., 42.

Democratic Futures

In February 2003, the president's post–9/11 popularity was in the low 60s, about where Bush 41's was before the eighteen-point increase afforded by the 1991 Persian Gulf War's rally effect. Bush 43 experienced fresh rally effects during the 2003 war against Iraq, but how, if at all, this might matter in 2004 relative to economic conditions and other determinants of election outcomes is anyone's guess.

But these imponderables aside, one searches in vain for evidence that Democrats are, in any case, ready to soar if Republicans stumble and the first-term president's popularity stalls and falls as his father's did. Let me offer just three examples.

The much-ballyhooed "Gingrich Revolution" ended within two years of the House GOP's plans to cut Medicare and other widely popular government programs created and defended by Democrats. True, but in February 2003, and without "boasting about the boldness" of its vision,[9] the Bush administration was advancing sweeping changes in both Medicare and Medicaid that were in many respects more radical than what Gingrich had proposed.

Governors' mansions remain pretty well split between the parties, while most big cities are still led by Democrats. Also true, but, at a moment of supreme fiscal stress for states and cities, the Bush administration is apparently in a strong enough position to dismiss out of hand doing anything like what most Demo-

[9] Robin Toner and Robert Pear, "Bush Proposes Major Changes in Medicare and Medicaid," *The New York Times*, February 24, 2003, A1.

cratic governors and mayors insist is necessary to address the crisis.[10]

Arguably, since 2000, Democrats have led on homeland security. Democrats such as Connecticut's Senator Joseph Lieberman called for a new department of homeland security nine months before the White House agreed that one was needed; Democratic governors like Pennsylvania's Ed Rendell have made homeland security a real state government priority; and Democratic mayors such as Baltimore's Martin O'Malley have issued impossible-to-rebut public criticisms of the federal homeland security effort to date. Fair enough. But while some political observers acknowledge Democratic leadership on homeland security, it is hardly a reality to most Americans. The same is true for Democratic leadership on lots of issues, new and old.

Finally, Democratic electoral futures will dim unless the party gets right with churchgoing religious voters and holds on to younger African-American voters. In 2000, Bush won huge majorities among churchgoing mainline Protestants, white evangelicals, and white Catholics, and the religion gap rivaled the gender gap (men favor Republicans, women favor Democrats) in electoral significance.[11] Between 2000 and 2002, Democratic identification among all black voters fell from 74 percent to 63 percent; among black voters ages twenty-six to thirty-five, it

---

[10] David Broder, "Stiffing States and Cities," *The Washington Post,* November 24, 2002, B7; Robert Pear, "Governors Get Sympathy from Bush but No More Money," *The New York Times,* February 25, 2003, A1.

[11] John C. Green, "Religion and Voting in the 2000 Elections," paper presented at the Center for Ethics and Public Policy, Washington, D.C., January 2001.

declined from 70 percent to 56 percent; and among black voters ages thirty-six to fifty, it dropped from 79 percent to 65 percent.[12] If Democrats continue to concede most religious voters while losing the solid support of black voters, then, in a phrase, and at least at the national level, the party is over.

[12] Data reported in Joint Center for Political and Economic Studies, *Focus: Political Report* (November/December 2002), 6.

Building a Nation
as Strong as Its Spirit

Senator John Edwards

The senior U.S. senator from North Carolina, JOHN EDWARDS is a leading Democratic candidate for president. The son of a mill worker and the first in his family to go to college, Edwards entered public service to represent the people he grew up with. His bipartisan accomplishments include strong and far-reaching patient-protection legislation, major investments in America's public schools, strong antiterrorism measures, and legislation to fight corporate corruption.

EVERY DAY ACROSS AMERICA, MOST PEOPLE GO TO WORK BELIEVing that hard work will earn them a chance to get ahead. From the biggest cities to the smallest towns, millions of Americans do everything they can to care for their children and prepare them for the future. Yet in spite of all these efforts, many parents find they just don't have the time or money to give their children the support they know they deserve. We can do better.

I grew up in Robbins, North Carolina, a small town in the Piedmont where my dad worked in the textile mills for thirty-six years. Working alongside my dad, I learned the values of hard work and perseverance. He taught me that anyone who works hard can achieve his or her dreams, and he taught me that all Americans deserve an equal opportunity to succeed and be heard. I was the first in my family to go to college and law school. And then I spent nearly twenty years as a lawyer fighting for the same people I'd grown up with, people who, like my own father, believed in the American dream that everyone deserves a chance to succeed in life. They are the reason I ran for the Senate. They are the reason I want to be president.

Most folks don't care much about Republicans or Democrats or the politics of Washington, D.C. They don't ask much from government, but what they do ask for means a lot. They want their leaders to honor their values, tell the truth, keep America safe and strong, listen to ordinary Americans, and give them half a chance to make the most of their God-given talents. They believe in an America that gives everyone a chance to get a good education and raise a healthy family. The American people deserve a government that believes in that, too.

For most Americans, September 11 was a sobering reminder of what matters most: family, faith, and country. And at a time when Americans are concerned with protecting and strengthening their families more than anything else, our government ought to make that a priority.

Parents raise our children, not the government, but we need to lend struggling families a hand. Today, 70 percent of kids do not have a stay-at-home parent, and parents now have twenty-two fewer hours to spend with their children every week than they did in 1969.

It should be a national goal to do far better by America's families. But that goal isn't enough. We need specific steps—and new ideas—to serve the families that make America great.

We should make sure parents struggling to raise their kids have the help they need to do it. I have proposed a refundable Family Leave Tax Credit of $2,500 for families with newborn children. This credit will give millions of families their first real chance to take time off when their child is born. My wife, Elizabeth, and I set up an after-school program in Raleigh, North Carolina, and we know firsthand how much good after-school opportunities can mean for children and parents. We need millions more opportunities like that.

In spite of *Brown v. Board of Education,* America still has two school systems—now divided more by income than by race. It defies everything our country stands for. We need to bring the best teachers into the poorest, most isolated school districts with better pay and scholarships. At the same time, we need to make sure that all teachers are held accountable.

The best thing we can do for families, of course, is get our economy going again, because good jobs are still the best family policy of all. I've proposed a plan to give our economy a shot in the arm now. But the most important step we can take to rejuvenate our economy is to get back to fiscal discipline over the long term. That means delaying the Bush tax cut for the wealthiest, but it also means eliminating spending that we don't need and can't afford. I've proposed cutting 10 percent of the federal workforce outside of national security over the next ten years. With these steps, we can save more than $1.6 trillion over the next twenty years—far more than the cost of any of the measures I've mentioned.

In the months after September 11, the American people have faced some tough times. I believe they've set an example to make us all proud. Americans feel a sense of common purpose and responsibility like nothing we've known in our lifetime. We need to harness that sense of responsibility, to build a nation as strong as our spirit. President Bush recently said that American spirit has never been stronger. I agree with that. But our job will not be done until we can say the same thing about the American Dream.

The Perspective of History

Professor Joseph Ellis

JOSEPH ELLIS *is a prominent American historian. His biography of* Thomas Jefferson, American Sphinx, *won the National Book Award. His* Founding Brothers *won the Pulitzer Prize.*

1. Is this an unusual time in our domestic political life?

Quite. It is highly unusual for one party to dominate all three branches of the government. The Republicans control and enjoy a slim conservative majority on the Supreme Court. This rarely happens. Even in the era of Democratic domination during the New Deal, the Supreme Court resisted FDR's magic.

For at least two reasons, I don't think this situation will last

long. First, our constitutional system is rigged in favor of balance—
the Founders designed it that way—so the abiding trend is toward
equilibrium. Second, power invariably goes to the heads of the
dominating party, for the same reason that indulged children
become spoiled and overweight. In short, the long-term historical pattern is clear and the current Republican hegemony is an
aberration within this pattern.

2. What do you think caused this aberration?

Nothing structural; that is, nothing with deep economic or demographic roots. If I were a smarter historian, perhaps I could identify some seismic shift, but I don't see any. Or perhaps it's more
correct to say that the different shifts offset one another. The continued migration to the Sun Belt favors the Republicans. But the
increased number of immigrants favors the Democrats. The Clinton boom of the 1990s significantly increased the wealth of the top
tier, a traditional Republican constituency, but it also sharpened
and widened class distinctions, which should provide ammuni-
tion to the Democrats. When you look at that famous color-coded
map of voting preferences in the presidential election of 2000, the
most literal interpretation is that Democrats breed near oceans
and rivers and Republicans prefer mountains and deserts. That's
obviously silly.

The chief source of the aberration, I think, is more immediate and temporary. It is September 11. This was the traumatic
event that threw an electromagnetic field over our national politics. By casting Bush in the role of commander in chief, it has
immunized his presidency against the customary criticisms and

extended the traditional six-month honeymoon into the indefinite future. It also seems to have paralyzed Democratic candidates in the midterm elections, permitting Republican gains in both the House and Senate that defied the historical pattern. The Republican ascendancy is really the Bush ascendancy, and it is almost exclusively a function of the fears generated by the terrorist threat.

3. Given the depth and extent of the public fears, why do you say that the current aberration is temporary?

Well, I think we are exaggerating and overreacting to the threat, are still under the traumatic spell of those horrible scenes of the World Trade Center and the Pentagon. On any sensibly constructed historical scale, September 11 does not constitute a viable threat to our national security comparable to several past threats. To be sure, lives and lifestyles are at risk, and duct tape will do little to protect them. But the survival of the American republic is not at risk. The magnitude of the threat posed by terrorists does not reach the same ominous threshold produced by the British military invasions during the American Revolution or the War of 1812, the sectional crisis of 1861, the totalitarian challenge posed by Germany and Japan in the 1930s and 1940s, or the communist threat of the Cold War era, which reached its most dangerous phase during the Cuban Missile Crisis in 1963. In all these previous episodes, failure meant the demise of the American republic as we know it.

We need to recover a sense of perspective. The Islamic fundamentalists can hurt us, but they cannot bring us down. To believe they can is to accept at face value their own fanatic rhetoric. I think we are living through a hyperbolic moment, that we are hyperventilating in a way that is distorting the normal breathing patterns of our political life.

4. If you're right about the limited character of the terrorist threat to our national security, what makes you confident that we will recover a sense of perspective?

Because the historical pattern, once again, suggests that is what happens. During the quasi-war with France in 1789 we passed the Alien and Sedition Acts. During the Civil War we abandoned habeas corpus. After World War I we deported and jailed recent immigrants. After Pearl Harbor we interred Japanese Americans. In the early years of the Cold War we believed Joseph McCarthy's rantings about communists in the State Department. (Though, truth be known, there were some, to include Alger Hiss.) In retrospect, all of those fear-gripped decisions have come to be regarded as embarrassing stains on our national reputation. To paraphrase Casey Stengel, you can look it up in any standard American history textbook. Some of the security-driven violations of the Bill of Rights currently sponsored by the Justice Department and the newly created Department of Homeland Security will eventually become fresh entries in this list of sincere but misguided excesses. The real question is not whether we will come to our senses, but how long it will take us to do so, and what damage we will do in the process.

5. Did I hear you correctly a little earlier when you seemed to say that the threat posed by Islamic terrorists should not be equated with the threat posed by communism in the Cold War?

My major point was that we tend to overreact to threats regardless of their origin. And we eventually regret it. But, yes, I do believe that we faced a more serious and ominous threat from Soviet communism during the cold war than we do now from Islamic terrorists.

One reason is the difference in destructive capability. The Soviets possessed the nuclear capability to annihilate the American population. In a worst-case scenario, the Islamic terrorists could detonate a dirty bomb in one American city. Another reason is the difference in what we might call ideological or political potency. Communism was a modern concept rooted in a utopian idea about social equality. It was an idea that failed spectacularly, especially in Stalin's version of the vision. Islamic fundamentalism, on the other hand, is a medieval concept rooted in the Dark Ages. It is a cri de coeur against modernity itself, based on a set of values that has long ago been swept into the dustbin of history. God's not on our side in this struggle, but history is. And we need to conduct ourselves with the calm confidence that follows from that realization.

6. Isn't what you call confidence a polite way of describing arrogance?

That all depends. It would be arrogant to believe that Jeffersonian democracy can be planted in Iraq and flourish because of its inherent superiority. It would be confident to assume that, when it comes to the much-discussed "clash of civilizations," the track record of Western institutions possesses decisive advantages.

7. Is racial diversity one of America's advantages?

Yes, and we need to remind ourselves how unusual and how recent our commitment to a multiracial society truly is. By unusual I mean that, in a global context, there are few major nations with

America's extensive racial mosaic. By recent I mean that the racial history of the United States did not endorse a biracial ideal until the middle of the twentieth century. And now, of course, it is a multiracial ideal. While I think it's understandable that we focus much of our social commentary on the gap between the ideal and reality, from both a global and historical perspective the salient and most conspicuous fact is our broadly shared commitment to racial equality. Neither China, Japan, Russia, nor the major European powers can match us on this score. And given the long-standing racist history of the United States, it is rather remarkable how much progress has occurred within the span of one or two generations. While it is fashionable, and probably useful, to describe this particular glass as still half-empty, we ought to periodically notice the striking achievement our half-full glass represents in the larger and longer context.

8. Does this longer perspective you speak of shed any special light on the character of our current political leadership?

Remember that our political system was designed to function as a government of laws rather than men. Monarchies and dictatorships are dependent on the personalities of their leaders. The American republic depends on the strength of its institutions. Bold leadership is not required, nor even encouraged, except in times of crisis. That is why the three great presidents in American history—Washington, Lincoln, and FDR—achieved greatness. They served at truly critical moments when the very fate of the nation was at stake. Otherwise we mistrust and usually discard political leaders who march too far ahead of public opinion.

My own sense is that President Bush has carried the Republican Party far to the right of the political center, where the majority of citizens and voters reside. He has managed to do this under the mantle of commander in chief and with the conviction—a sincere conviction—that the survival of the nation is at risk. As indicated earlier, I think he is wrong about that. And as the crisis atmosphere recedes, the political implications of his conservative domestic agenda and his unilateral foreign policy initiative will cause serious problems for the Republican Party, because the clear majority of American voters oppose his tax cuts and his redefinition of America's role in the world. If anything, Bush has been too much of a leader, for he has taken us to a place where only a minority of Americans wish to go. As the patriotic fervor that understandably accompanied our military invasion of Iraq recedes, the fiscal and international wreckage generated by his policies will become more starkly visible.

The hallmark of political leadership in the aftermath of this quasi crisis will be the courage to ask for sacrifice. Neither of the two political parties has demonstrated much courage on this score in recent years, preferring to encourage the illusion that we can have guns and butter, war and tax cuts, environmental protection and economic development, international support and superpower arrogance. As these bills come due over the ensuing years, true American statesmanship will come to depend on the simple talent for straight talk, a rare commodity in any political season.

9. Beyond a measure of candor, does history offer any guidance about the domestic and foreign policy directions in which prospective leaders should lead us?

History is a bit like the Delphic oracle. The wisdom she speaks is invariably ambiguous, and anyone who hears a clear message had best listen again. On the domestic side, the voices I hear tell me that the incredible wealth generated by the hegemony of the United States in the global marketplace has created the kind of social and economic gap between rich and poor last seen in the Gilded Age. The Bush tax policies have only exacerbated this trend. If leadership is going where history wants or needs to go, the proper direction is toward closing the gap.

On the foreign policy side, the Bush doctrine post–September 11 has embraced a unilateral and preemptive definition of American power in the world. From the Roman Empire of classical antiquity to the British Empire of the modern era, this is the fatal mistake, usually called overreach. Except for Vietnam, we had managed to avoid this mistake during the first fifty years of American imperial hegemony. In the end, all empires have limited life spans, but the best way to extend the duration of the American Empire is to make it less rather than more imperial in its mode of conduct. The Bush foreign policy since September 11 points us in the opposite direction and toward an agenda of global peacekeeping that cannot be sustained. The moment in which we are currently living is a hubristic bubble destined to burst before long. And when it does, leadership will mean reengagement with Europe in creating an international agenda in which our unprecedented power is less conspicuous and more consensual. In the long run, as Lord Keynes quipped, we are all dead. But partnering our power is the only way to prolong the American chapter in world history.

Winning Big with Youth: A Democratic Strategy of New Ideas

Andrew J. Frank and Joel C. Washington

ANDREW J. FRANK, *from Glen Ellyn, Illinois, is a graduate of Glenbard West High School.* JOEL C. WASHINGTON, *from Silver Spring, Maryland, is a graduate of Gonzaga College High School. Both are on the Harvard College Democrats Executive Board and will graduate with the class of 2005.*

OVER THE COURSE OF THE LAST CENTURY, THE STRENGTH OF THE Democratic Party has rested with its ability to challenge the status quo and offer Americans, especially young Americans, new ideas and a purpose greater than their own. Woodrow Wilson gave the nation an idealistic vision of peace through international cooperation. Franklin Roosevelt won in 1932 by promising a "New Deal" that transformed the role of government in the lives of Americans. John F. Kennedy won in 1960 by communicating a vision of American greatness through youthful energy. Lyndon Johnson handily defeated his opponent, Barry Goldwater, in 1964 by offering the "Great Society" that ingrained the fundamental notion that Americans are responsible for the care of the most fragile citizens. Jimmy Carter defeated Gerald Ford in 1976 by offering a respite from the corruption, stagnation, and elitism of Ford and Nixon through a new era of open government and strong moral leadership. And Bill Clinton beat George H. W. Bush by rejecting the Reaganomics of the past twelve years and presenting innovative, energetic, and ambitious ideas for the twenty-first-century economy.

Yet current Democrats, whether liberal, moderate, conservative, or "no label," break from their party's history: they have no new ideas to excite voters. Consider the issues of the day: *National Security.* Republicans have offered a new vision for the post–September 11 world: preemption founded upon American power. Democrats talked about multilateralism and containment— the policies of the past. *Fiscal Policy.* Republicans have offered sweeping tax cuts for an overregulated economy, while Democrats have proposed more moderate tax relief. *Education.* Republicans have proposed new measures of accountability and choice for America's failing schools, while Democrats reaffirm their belief in public education. *Social Security and Health Care.* Republicans warn of impending collapse due to demographic shifts, and offer new market-based solutions. Democrats argue that the current system should be preserved.

As we can see, the Democrats had a message: "Me too, but not as much." They also had ideas, the only problem being they were old, stale, and rehashed. Neither of these fully explains why Democrats lost in 2002. They lost because, on each issue important to Americans, they took the Republican policy as the starting point for debate and offered a moderate version of the same policy. By offering new ideas, Republicans put Democrats on the defensive and set the terms of debate; Democrats allowed themselves to be defined by what they opposed rather than what they advocated.

So where should the Democratic Party go? Presidential candidate Joe Lieberman represents the centrist wing of the Democratic Party that argues for more moderate versions of Republican plans. Another candidate, Howard Dean, represents the liberal wing that argues that we should respond to Bush's plans with more expanded versions of past policies. Other Democratic candidates fall in the middle of this political spectrum. Yet the choice between liberal and moderate fundamentally misses the point. The future success of the Democratic Party does not rest on whether they move to the left or the right; it depends on whether they move forward. Democrats must reclaim their identity as the proponents of new ideas instead of as the defenders of old ideas.

Democrats must offer a new vision that is not in response to Republican policies, but in response to the challenges that lie ahead. Democrats need policies that will excite and unite Americans, rather than divide and embitter them. Only then can Democrats bring in young and disillusioned Americans. To accomplish this feat, Democrats have to transcend ideology and appeal to

America's unique sense of hope. This will create a national consciousness, similar to the American spirit inspired by World War II, the space race, and the Olympics, that will position the Democratic Party as a uniting entity of the future.

Democrats must become a party that invests in technology to prevent agroterrorism, detects portable nuclear weapons, and inoculates against deadly bacteria to ensure homeland security; a party that makes health insurance as common as car insurance; a party that promises to put an American on Mars by the end of the decade; a party that starts with the integration of security into the Department of Homeland Security and continues to fuse old bureaucracies into a newer, more efficient, more modern government; a party that pushes a large-scale effort for the development and application of energy technologies upon which the twenty-first century's economy will depend; a party that promises to elevate a quality education to the level of a *right* to which every child is entitled; a party that is defined by its forward-looking goals rather than its transitory policies; a party that fundamentally will not be told what it cannot accomplish. This is the Democratic Party of the twenty-first century, a party that will bring out the energy and vigor of Americans.

These big ideas will also bring out young Americans. From civil rights to human rights, to the environment and beyond, young Americans always lead the fight, because they know that the victories will be long lasting and broad in scope. Young people, in general, look for a sense of meaning, for a cause greater than themselves; this selfless idealism can be invigorated by Democrats through the political process. It is no accident that when

President John F. Kennedy asked Americans, "Ask not what your country can do for you; ask what you can do for your country," young people responded. These days, we see a young generation of Americans that, more so than any other, selflessly gives their time to volunteer in their communities, across the country, and around the world. Our leaders must channel this energy toward the challenges of the twenty-first century.

The Democratic Party is uniquely poised to offer new ideas and attract young voters because it always has been *the* party to do so. It was Democrats who championed government activism in the economy to counter the Great Depression. It was Democrats who brought about the modern Civil Rights movement, ending the most shameful practices of voter discrimination in American history. It was Democrats who spurred the environmental movement, saving uncountable lives and preserving our irreplaceable resources. It was Democrats who had the strength of character to lead America through two world wars. It was Democrats who provided a security net for all Americans, to relieve the abject poverty that afflicted so many. It was Democrats who elevated human rights to the same level as American security. Democrats have always offered the big ideas needed to confront big challenges, and these are the ideas that young Americans care about. Democrats today, if they wish to be relevant in the next hundred years, must take on grand challenges. They must move from interest-group politics to movement politics, and in the process transform the national consciousness.

When Republicans offer new ideas, they put Democrats on the defensive and force them to defend old ideas. Conservatives can win elections by defending the status quo; Democrats cannot.

Democrats should quit talking about stale ideas and incremental change and start offering new, proactive stances that take into account the realities of the twenty-first century. If they do so, they will win big in elections, win big with youth, and once again lead America through a new century.

Why Democrats Lost

Al From and Bruce Reed

AL FROM *is founder and CEO and* BRUCE REED *is president of the Democratic Leadership Council.*

TWO YEARS OF ONE-PARTY RULE WON'T BE GOOD FOR THE COUNtry, nor as good for President Bush and the Republicans as their celebrations after the 2002 elections suggest. But as much as it hurts right now, the pasting Democrats took in the midterms could prove to be a blessing in disguise for the party. If Democrats learn the right lessons from defeat—admittedly a big if—their party and the country will be better for it down the road.

AL FROM AND BRUCE REED

Democrats are always good at making excuses, and as usual they have plenty today. Since 9/11, President Bush has remained far more popular with the American people than his policies merit. It's not easy making inroads in times of war against a popular president and a politically savvy White House. This election was fought on their turf and their terms.

But let's face it: the last two years have been the worst period for Democrats in at least two decades. The midterm report card on the party is grim: for two years now, Democrats have had too little to say and been too timid to say it.

That is not an ideological statement, nor an attempt to point fingers. Centrist Democrats who hid behind the president's tax cut are as guilty as traditional Democrats who hid behind the same Social Security attack ads they've been running for twenty years. Democratic candidates forgot the cardinal rule of American politics: you can't win an argument unless you make one.

This isn't the first time Democrats have hit the hustings only to discover they had nothing to offer. In 1988, the epitaph on the Dukakis campaign was, "Don't just stand there—say something!" In the run-up to the 1994 midterm elections, congressional leaders and Democratic strategists made a fateful decision to attack the Contract with America, rather than offer an alternative reform vision.

Shortly after the 1994 debacle, President Clinton said, "The voters handed us a good country licking. They were sending us a message to get done what we promised." The next two years were the most successful of his presidency, because he resolved to make a clear case for progress to the American people, not simply mind-meld with the Democratic caucus in Congress. The strength of his ideas enabled Clinton to help his party climb out of a much deeper hole than the one we're in now.

The question for 2004 is whether the party will learn its lesson again. Democrats have a better approach on economic growth, expanding opportunity, and keeping the country safe. But for the second straight election, they made the case *against* the GOP plan instead of *for* their own—and as a result did worse than the mood of the country would indicate. For voters, the choice in this election was thin gruel: Democrats attacked the Republican agenda; Bush attacked Democrats for blocking it.

The party's problem on Election Day 2002 wasn't ideology; it was ideas. In a Gallup Poll taken just after the election only 30 percent of the voters said Democrats had a clear plan to cure the nation's ills. Half the voters thought the Republicans did.

Here are five lessons Democrats can learn from this election.

Democrats need to appeal to all Americans, not narrow interests. The Democratic message was a tired appeal to groups, with little more to offer than prescription drugs and the status quo on Social Security. That message was too easily neutralized by Republicans saying they were against privatization of Social Security and for prescription drugs, too. For all their kvetching on Social Security, Democrats lost the senior vote.

Democrats need to expand their base, not just to energize it. Of course, Democrats should go all out to rally their faithful to the polls, but that can't be the end of their strategy. The Democratic base just isn't big enough to win. The harsh reality is that there are more conservatives than liberals (and more moderates than either), more Independents than either Democrats or Republicans, more suburbanites than big-city dwellers, more whites than minorities, more nonunion workers than union workers.

Contrary to conventional wisdom, moving left is counterproductive. Voters already think Democrats are too far left. In a postelection Gallup Poll, 39 percent of all Americans said the Democrats were too liberal, and 54 percent of Democrats said their party needs to moderate its liberal message.

In 2004, Democrats must win the swing voters in the political center. Those voters tend to be white, politically moderate, loosely tied if at all to a political party, living in the suburbs, and working in nonunion jobs. Democrats ignore them at their own peril because they can't win without them. Clinton, with his New Democrat message, won overwhelmingly in the cities—and in twenty-four of the twenty-eight largest suburban counties. Democrats can rally their base and win swing voters, too.

Democrats need to get the big things right. That means national security and the economy. The president's first responsibility is as commander in chief. Right now, by huge margins voters trust Republicans over Democrats on national security and fighting terrorism. According to a postelection Gallup survey, 57 percent of Americans think that Democrats are not tough enough on terrorism; 64 percent said the Republicans are tough enough. Democrats simply can't let those perceptions stand. The Democratic nominee in 2004 must convince voters that he'll keep them safe. If he doesn't, nothing else will matter.

President Bush's economic record leaves him vulnerable. But, to take advantage, Democrats need to offer a credible plan for growing the economy. Trimming the tax cut makes sense, but as part of a comprehensive Democratic alternative that includes their own tax cuts and ideas for increasing investment, creating jobs, raising incomes, and expanding opportunity. Once the Democrats earn voter confidence on national security and the economy, voters will listen to all the other good things they have to say.

Democrats need to offer bold, innovative reforms, not incremental change. A bold tax overhaul would be a start. And there are plenty of other big challenges in search of big ideas: the aging of America and the baby boom retirement; exploding health costs, insuring the uninsured, and providing long-term care; balancing work and family; and achieving energy independence. If Democrats tackle these challenges with approaches President Bush can't co-opt, voters will reward them.

Democrats need to look outside Washington for answers. We have a great opportunity to do this with the increased number of Democratic governors. In Washington, Democratic activists tend to think in terms of interests and constituencies. That's why for practical ideas that work Democrats ought to look to their leaders who live outside of Washington and are held accountable for what they do. Americans don't want a party that speaks for organized interest groups. They want a party that tackles problems with practical solutions and speaks with a clear sense of national purpose.

In 2004, Democrats can be that party. If they are, they'll recapture the vital center and Americans will once again turn to them for national leadership.

Democrats had, and still have, a winning case to make. It's

not better tactics, stronger turnout, or please, God, tougher at-tack ads. It's not rushing out to reopen all the doubts Democrats worked so hard to put behind them in the '90s. All Democrats have to do is let the country know how much they can get done, instead of how much they'll stop. That will surprise everyone—and it just might be enough to win.

A Fourth Way for Democrats

Congressman Dick Gephardt

The son of a Teamster and a secretary, DICK GEPHARDT represents the Third Congressional District of Missouri and is a candidate for president of the United States. Gephardt, an accomplished lawmaker and leader in Congress for more than two decades, has worked his entire public life for economic growth and increased opportunity for all Americans.

IT'S GETTING HARDER TO RAISE A STRONG FAMILY IN AMERICA. There are more and more families where both parents work, just to pay the bills; where parents rarely share meals with their own children; where it's a struggle to pass on the right values, to teach simple lessons of discipline and respect, right and wrong. Parents shouldn't lie awake at night, wondering if a doctor's bill or a mortgage payment is going to break their bank account.

Many in the Republican Party believe in survival of the fittest, in feeding those at the top and hoping some crumbs fall off the table. I believe that if we reward the work and initiative of ordinary Americans, if we empower them and enable them to prosper, then everybody benefits, from the factory floor to the corporate boardroom.

We can't be satisfied until every family, not just the few, can share in the bounty of America. We can't be satisfied until we've made opportunity real for everyone who's willing to work for it. That's the crusade Democrats must undertake to win the White House and Congress in 2004. We must offer a vision to lift this lagging economy and build a new American prosperity.

Ten years ago, America was at another economic crossroads. We were losing jobs, incomes were falling, and our nation was choked with the highest deficits in history. As House majority leader, I led the fight to pass the Clinton-Gore economic plan to slash the deficit, invest in education, cut taxes for working families, and ask the wealthy to pay their fair share.

Not a single Republican voted for that plan. They said it was a job-killer. Instead, it led to the single longest economic expansion in history, the highest rate of home ownership ever, the lowest inflation in a generation, and more than 22 million new jobs. Turns out we were right and they were wrong. They should have learned a lesson: that huge, budget-busting tax cuts for the wealthiest do not educate a single child, extend health coverage to a single family, or create a single job.

Yet President Bush has taken us right back to the broken policies of the past, the economics of debt and regret: unaffordable tax cuts for the few. We are left a nation with zero job creation, racked with debt, unprepared for the economy of the future. We are left a nation that's growing apart, when we should be growing together.

Democrats must seize on the fact that President Bush has no plan to get this economy moving again. At the dawn of the global economy and Information Age, we cannot afford to wait. At a time when world markets are getting more competitive—when we need to be leaner, smarter, more innovative than ever—we cannot afford four more years of Bush economics. Democrats must develop an economic plan that works for everybody—with real job creation, real skills development, real help for hardworking families. We must replace an agenda of division and exclusion, and fight for the American family again.

I believe there's a new way to achieve that fundamental purpose—a fourth way, if you will. Not government handouts, not tax cuts for the few, and not just focusing on incremental solutions, as important as that's been—but taking major steps to give people the tools of true self-reliance.

We must recast our party's goals for a new economy, a new age. We must fight for tax credits that guarantee every worker health coverage and pensions they can take with them everywhere they work. We must aspire to hire 2.5 million new, quality teachers over the next ten years. We must strive to become energy independent in the next decade by launching an Apollo Project to develop new, cleaner technologies.

After 9/11, we can no longer vie to be the majority party without directly addressing national security and homeland security concerns. We must start with an unshakable commitment to keep our defenses strong. We're in a new world, with manifold new dangers—from global terror, to the recklessness of rogue dictators like Saddam Hussein, to international crime and drug-running that rip at the very fabric of freedom.

We must pledge that our armed forces remain the best-equipped, best-trained, best-led fighting force in the entire world. We need a twenty-first-century military—capable of rooting out and combating terrorism and all other threats to our well-being, at home and abroad.

I stood with this administration's efforts to disarm Saddam Hussein. But, for all our military might, we must remember that there are too many threats to our security, too many global challenges for America to simply go it alone. We need the friendship and cooperation of our time-honored allies. We must lead the world, instead of merely bullying it.

America has a mission that's unique in human history—to prove that liberty and democracy are indivisible, the birthright of all people everywhere. If we can do more to share democratic values, then we won't have to rely on arms alone.

And we must do more to ensure the security of our homeland where it matters most—in the places where you live and work. When we tried to add billions for security at airports and energy plants, Republicans in Congress said no. When we tried to help local law enforcement protect us in our homes and our neighborhoods, the president threatened a veto.

Democrats should demand that we give local police and fire departments, the first responders, unprecedented tools and training, so they can be the front line in the war against terror.

Let's be clear. Democrats shouldn't ask Americans to do what's easy. We must ask them to do what's hard. It's easy to give a quick tax break to a corporation, so it has higher profits for the next quarter. It's hard to modernize our education system, so that corporation has a smarter, better-educated workforce for the next century.

Dr. Martin Luther King taught us that we are all "tied in a single garment of destiny. Whatever affects one directly, affects all indirectly." As he once said, "I can never be what I ought to be until you are what you ought to be."

We're all bound together. If a child doesn't have health insurance, we all pay the price when she shows up at the emergency room. If a child drops out of school and joins a gang, or goes on welfare, we all pay the price of violence, dependence, and indigence. If a family can't afford to put a child through college, we all pay the price of sinking productivity, of shattered human potential.

We can take that fight to the American people and we can win. We can build an America where we grow together instead of being pulled apart—where our economy's strong because all our families are secure—where nobody's left out or left behind.

Al Franken and a Few
Other Reasons I'm No Longer
a Democrat

Bernard Goldberg

BERNARD GOLDBERG *is the winner of seven Emmy Awards and was once rated by* TV Guide *one of the ten most interesting people on television. Having served for nearly thirty years as a reporter and producer for CBS News, he now reports for the critically acclaimed HBO program* Real Sports, *hosted by Bryant Gumbel. He is the author of the bestselling book* Bias. *Goldberg has written op-eds for* The New York Times, The Wall Street Journal, *and* The Washington Post. *He lives with his family in Miami.*

As I WRITE THIS IN MARCH 2003, SEVERAL WEALTHY DEMOCRATIC fund-raisers are trying to start a liberal radio talk show network.

As you read this, the effort may have already failed. If it hasn't yet, it will.

The thinking behind the venture is simple: Democrats feel that in the 2002 elections they weren't able to get their message out, which is why they suffered such a stunning defeat. A liberal radio talk network, they reason, would counter the influence of conservative talk radio and Fox News and *The Washington Times*, which Democrats like Al Gore believe are pretty much wholly owned subsidiaries of the Republican Party.

Apparently it hasn't occurred to Democrats that if they had indeed gotten their message out—louder, clearer, and to more people—there's a good chance they would have lost even bigger than they did. Apparently it hasn't occurred to them that maybe it was the message that the voters rejected. Nor has it occurred to them that this notion that the big bad conservative media are silencing them is downright laughable—literally. In fact, one night Jay Leno said, "A group of venture capitalists are in the process of developing their own liberal radio network to counter conservative shows like Rush Limbaugh. They feel the liberal viewpoint is not being heard—except on TV, in the movies, in music, by comedians, in magazines and newspapers. Other than that, it's not getting out." The joke got a great big laugh, which is telling since the audience wasn't made up of the Young Conservative Right Wing Nut Republicans of America—just your regular Middle American types. You think maybe just about *everybody* by now thinks it's funny when the Left complains that "the liberal viewpoint is not being heard"?

But what isn't so funny is the important lesson in all of this for the Democratic Party. Liberal talk radio in the past has failed, and will fail again, because the American people don't think they need yet another media megaphone coming from left field. The Left, of course, has another explanation: conservatives, they say, are loud and angry and make complex issues moronically simple for all those moronically simple conservatives in the Red States. Never mind that the analysis is shamelessly self-serving; what's far more important is that it too easily dismisses those people in the Red States, some of whom the Democrats might actually win over if they respected them and listened to them and weren't stereotyping them as zombielike conservative dolts who will do anything Rush Limbaugh tells them to do.

But here's the part the Democrats really need to pay attention to: the success of conservative talk shows isn't just about America's disaffection with the liberal media; it's about America's disaffection with liberalism itself: with liberals' abiding respect for diversity (except, of course, diversity of opinion); with their reflexive tendency to blame America first for whatever is wrong in the world; with their deep suspicion of America's military; with their monumental hypocrisy (as in their enthusiastic support of affirmative action, as long as it doesn't adversely affect their own kids); with their self-righteous support for "art" seemingly designed to do nothing more than offend sensible people, often sensible people of faith. Remember "Piss Christ" and that other "masterpiece" that portrayed the Virgin Mary surrounded by elephant dung?

This is why liberal talk on television and radio has failed, why Phil Donahue and Mario Cuomo and Jerry Brown and Jim

Hightower and a bunch of others are no longer on the air. And it's why the next Great Liberal Hope, whoever that turns out to be, will fall on his (or her) face, too. And far more important, it's also why liberalism in our culture—once such a great American treasure—has lost so much of its luster over the years. And yes, it's why the Democratic Party—the liberal party in our country—has lost its luster, too.

By way of full disclosure, I grew up in a rock-solid blue-collar Democratic family. Everybody in the neighborhood was a Democrat. The older folks thought that FDR, who had trouble walking on land, could walk on water; and the kids loved JFK. I voted for George McGovern twice—once in my state's primary and once in the general election—and I didn't vote for Ronald Reagan even once. So it's not as if I'm some right-wing ideologue who detests the Democrats. I don't. But I do detest Democratic pandering and how that pandering has transformed a once great political party.

When I was in college I believed deeply that racial discrimination was immoral, as I still do. And I also believed, as I still do, that it's wrong to hire people based on the color of their skin. Back in college that was the progressive—the liberal—position. Today, the Democrats support what they call affirmative action, but what is really a system of racial preferences. Today Democrats support hiring people, at least in part, based on the color of their skin and admitting them into college for the same reason—and we're now supposed to accept that *that* is the enlightened, progressive position?

I happen to be pro-choice, but I have reservations. I don't think a young girl, who would get kicked out of school if she were caught with an unauthorized aspirin, should be allowed to get an abortion without the consent of at least one of her parents. And I don't think it should be legal to abort a fetus just days or weeks before it would otherwise become a living baby, except in the direst of circumstances. Yet it is Democrats who go to the most extreme wing of the abortion lobby—the wing that says there should be no restrictions at all on abortion—and beg for their support. Politicians who have opposed abortion on moral grounds their entire adult lives suddenly see the light—they've "evolved," they tell us—and become abortion rights supporters, the very second they decide to run for national office. I understand that we won't find many profiles in courage in the world of politics, but this fire sale of principles in exchange for a few votes is truly disgraceful.

If the Democrats keep it up they will set their party back fifty or sixty years. Which actually would be a great thing. Fifty or sixty years ago it was a party we could be proud of.

And one more thing: when modern Democrats talk about their wonderful coalition somehow I'm always left out. Democrats loved me when I was making $17,000 a year and paying almost nothing in taxes. Now I'm one of the villains "in the top 1 percent" who, as they see it, "doesn't *need* a tax cut" and doesn't pay his "fair share."

I understand how politics works. Democrats figure if they wage class warfare—if they portray that top 1 percent as a privileged few who already have too much—maybe then they can win over a majority of the other supposedly envious 99 percent. Once upon a time, cynical conservative politicians tried to divide Americans based on race. Today, cynical liberals try to turn people against each other based on class. Things like this may work in the short run, but they never work over the long haul. Americans are too decent to fall for it.

And here's the bottom line for the Democratic Party. I'm not alone. There are millions who don't like any of this, who don't like what the Democratic Party has become. Make that tens of millions. We feel betrayed. We have not deserted the Democratic Party. The Democratic Party has deserted us.

But in the end we all make decisions in life and we have to live with the consequences. Democrats have decided to allow the left wing of their party to call the shots, on everything from abortion and affirmative action to war and peace.

I wish them luck. They're going to need it.

Opportunity for All

Senator Bob Graham

BOB GRAHAM has dedicated his life to public service, and his constituents have recognized that commitment: he has never lost an election. After two terms in the state House of Representatives and two terms in the state Senate, Graham was elected the thirty-eighth governor of Florida in 1978. After two successful terms as governor, he was elected to the United States Senate in 1986 by defeating an incumbent Republican. He has been reelected to the Senate twice, in 1992 and 1998. He is now campaigning to become the forty-fourth president of the United States. He has been married to the former Adele Khoury of Miami Shores for forty-four years. They have four adult daughters and ten grandchildren.

WE STAND AT A CRITICAL TIME IN OUR NATION'S HISTORY.

President Bush took office at a time of unparalleled prosperity and historic budget surpluses—when America counted itself not only the strongest but also the most admired nation in the world.

Today, we live in a very different America. The stock market has lost one-quarter of its value, two million more Americans are jobless, 1.4 million more of us lack health insurance, budget surpluses have turned into the deepest deficits in history, and our country is viewed with increased hostility, not just by those who hate and threaten America but even by those who share our values.

We need leadership willing to fight for our nation's economic future instead of the short-term interests of a special few. We need leadership willing to consider solutions besides tax cuts for the rich.

We need a new playbook. If we're going to provide tax relief, let's give it to the people who work hard and play by the rules instead of another massive tax cut for the wealthiest Americans. If we're going to cut taxes, let's cut the payroll tax so every American who works benefits from tax relief.

And we should pay for it by going after those companies who moved offshore to avoid paying U.S. taxes and by closing other loopholes that allow big corporations to avoid paying taxes while most Americans foot the bill.

It is time to bring America back from one of our longest economic slowdowns ever. It is painfully clear the president has no idea how to lead us back to economic prosperity. We need a president who will bring America back—back to economic health, with policies that invest in our people and their future.

It is time to bring America back to an emphasis on protecting our *own* citizens. The Bush administration has ignored homeland security in all but name while it focused all its energy on Iraq. I know, as former chairman of the Senate Intelligence Committee, how little has been done to provide real security at home while our attention has been directed away to the War on Terror abroad.

It is time to bring America back together. President Bush sought office claiming to be a uniter not a divider, but he has pursued a divisive domestic agenda. He has talked the language of diversity and opportunity—but walked away from doing anything to promote them. As their friends at corporations like Enron pillaged the economy and the retirement hopes of millions of Americans, as the stock market's fall robbed even more millions of their savings, as executives raised their own salaries while firing workers, the Bush administration has answered with damning indifference. They have divided our nation between the few at the top, whom they serve, and the many, who are left to fend for themselves with help from our government that is no more than the moral equivalent of duct tape.

We have increasingly become two Americas.

I am running for president to bring back our economy. As Florida governor, I led in the creation of more than one million new jobs, invested in Florida's housing and infrastructure, and still kept the tax burden one of the lowest in the nation. As a senator, I helped pass an expansion of the Earned Income Tax Credit, tax breaks for small businesses, and tax deductions to help pay for college tuition. As president, I will revive the economy with needed investments in infrastructure and education, and with targeted tax cuts. I will pass on to our children and grandchildren a strong and growing economy, not a burden of debt.

I am running for president to bring back a focus on America's security. In the Senate, I helped lead the fight to mandate the first federal security standards for our nation's ports, spearheaded the investigation of 9/11, and, even before that tragedy, started the process of strengthening and reforming our intelligence agencies. As president, I will make sure homeland defense consists of more than just plastic wrap.

I am running for president to bring back America's commitment to protecting our families' health, promoting our children's education, and preserving our environmental heritage. As governor, I raised education standards, increased accountability and teacher salaries, and built new schools. I've worked across party lines to craft a bipartisan Medicare prescription drug plan that helps seniors, not the drug companies. I've launched efforts to save our Everglades, our coasts and beaches, our scenic and wild rivers, and our wetlands.

We need leaders who listen to the people of America instead of to the voices of ideological extremists.

I've spent my life listening to the voices of America. I've spent it working with America's people. I've worked construction, and taught in our schools. I've worked as a short-order cook, a security guard, and a truck driver. I've worked on the docks and on assembly lines.

I've been working side-by-side with Americans, in their everyday jobs, for twenty-five years. I've done almost four hundred workdays. It has helped me to better understand what Americans go through every day of their lives. Working these jobs has helped me to become a better public servant and a better person.

For me, working with Americans has meant learning from Americans. At a time when we have a president who does not share most Americans' problems and concerns but instead favors special interests, that experience exemplifies the values to which we must return.

My father was a dairy farmer. He taught me how to work hard and how to value a dollar. He taught me how to work the land—and how to love it. My mother, my wife, and two of my daughters have all been teachers. They have constantly reminded me of the importance of education and of opportunity to each and every child—to all Americans.

I have ten grandchildren, and I don't want theirs to be the first generation of Americans to inherit a country worse off than it was before. I am going to do everything I can to leave them a safer America, a more secure America, and a more prosperous America than it is today.

This election is about their future—and the futures of every child, in every town and city, in every family across America.

And that is why we must beat George W. Bush in 2004.

Where Do Democrats Go from Here? New Leadership, New Faces, or New Direction?

Congressman Jesse L. Jackson, Jr.

Congressman JESSE L. JACKSON, JR. (D-IL-2), was first elected to Congress in a special election on December 12, 1995, so this is his fifth term (104th to 108th Congress). He serves on the House Appropriations Committee. He is married to Sandi and has one child, a daughter, Jessica Donatella. He is thirty-eight (March 11, 1965). He, along with Frank E. Watkins, recently wrote, A More Perfect Union—Advancing New American Rights, *where he advocates putting the affirmative right to vote, right to an education of equal high quality, and the right to health care of equal high quality in the Constitution as new amendments.*

On Tuesday, November 5, 2002, Democrats lost and Republicans won. Both deserved what they got!

President Bush risked his political capital by campaigning strongly in swing races, and it paid high dividends. Democrats were divided on central issues, and were ineffective in offering an alternative and coherent vision to the Bush-Republican agenda.

Where are Democrats today?

There is a debate within the Democratic Party over what to do. How do we reconcile the conservative/moderate and liberal wings of the party? What should our message be?

Some suggest the party needs new leaders and new faces. I believe the issue for Democrats—and America—is not a new leader or face, but a new direction.

Both wings of the Democratic Party agree we need a change. The only question is: What's the change we need?

The 2002 midterm election gave a rationale and a justification to both sides. One wing said, "We're still seen as the 'tax and spend' party." The other wing said, "We're still perceived as being too much like the Republicans." As a result, each wing wants to go more and stronger in the direction they're already headed.

In 2000, 50 million Americans voted for George W. Bush and 50.5 million voted for Al Gore. As a result—using math I could only learn from the U.S. Supreme Court—George Bush won.

The strategic challenge is not, "How do we redivide the 100 million who voted?" but "How do we appeal to the 100 million who didn't vote, without completely alienating the 100 million who did?"

Personality is important. We do have to feel secure and comfortable with the people we vote for and elect. However, the present Democratic strategy is too narrow. The present strategy is to hook our wagon to a personality—Howard Dean, John Kerry, John Edwards, Joe Lieberman, Richard Gephardt, Al Sharpton, or others who may emerge. But "personality" is not the same as an idea or a vision big enough to cover all of the Democratic Party's constituents and interests.

"Who" is a secondary consideration. Over time, personalities will come and go. Of deeper concern is having the capacity to: (a) change the current political climate; (b) organize the broadest possible Democratic base; (c) unify the two wings of the party; and (d) do it for a very long time.

The answer is *not* a personality. It's *not* a conservative or a liberal policy. It's *not* a new legislative program. No, none of those things can accomplish these goals. *Only* a new material *right that will positively affect people's daily lives has the power to both maintain and expand the Democratic Party's base—and sustain it for a very long time!*

We are preoccupied with *party* (Democrats are right and Republicans are wrong); preoccupied with *ideology* (liberalism versus conservatism); and preoccupied with *policy* and *program* (a prescription drug benefit, a patient's bill of rights, raising the minimum wage, more money for the "Leave No Child Behind" program, all of which I support). But none of these preoccupations truly represents a new direction. None can bring both wings of the party together. And none represents an idea big enough or a vision strong enough to broaden our base and sustain it over time.

I recommend a strategy that has the broadest possible appeal for both wings of the Democratic Party; a strategy that has the best chance of energizing the 100 million voters and nonvoters; a strategy that can potentially bring young and old, middle class and working class, white and nonwhite, the educated and the less educated, the better-off and the poorest among us to the polls. It's not about personality, a party, an ideology, a policy, or a legislative program. It's about fighting for *rights*!

Democrats—conservatives, moderates, liberals, progressives, and populists—believe in all the right things; they just don't believe enough. They don't believe in them enough to fight for them as *rights*!

At the 1948 Democratic convention Hubert Humphrey gave Democrats the right advice. He said: "It is time for the Democratic Party to step out of the shadow of states' rights into the sunlight of human rights."

The *union* of the United States was built, rooted, and is held together by the Constitution. When Attorney General John Ashcroft tries to weaken the rights of the American people, our most fundamental appeal is not to a politician, but to our Constitution.

More positively, almost all of the major "progressive movements" in our country have been about the Constitution, either directly or indirectly—the African-American movement, the progressive tax movement, the democracy movement, the women's movement.

The abolitionist movement concluded with the Thirteenth Amendment, ending slavery; the Fourteenth Amendment, guaranteeing equal protection under the law and due process, and the Fifteenth Amendment, outlawing discrimination in voting on the basis of race.

The progressive taxation movement's logical conclusion was the Sixteenth Amendment.

One dimension of the ongoing democracy movement culminated in the Seventeenth Amendment—the direct election of U.S. senators.

The women's movement's goal was the Nineteenth Amendment—outlawing discrimination in voting on the basis of sex.

Outrage over young people being asked to fight in Vietnam at the age of eighteen when they were excluded from voting till age twenty-one resulted in the Twenty-sixth Amendment, an antidiscrimination amendment for everyone over age eighteen.

Virtually all of the major progressive movements in our history looked to and targeted the Constitution as an aid or a solution—and the Constitution impacts all Americans, not just those who vote. *Thus, by definition, a new right in the Constitution is not a special interest.*

Let me go a little deeper into the post–Civil War amendments. The word *slavery* never appeared in the Constitution—though the document addressed the institution in five different places. However, the Tenth Amendment says that any right not in the Constitution is reserved for the states. Slavery was not in the Constitution, so it was a "state right." Thus, the Constitution didn't *directly* protect "slavery," it protected the *slave system indirectly* through *"states' rights."*

Likewise, the institution of slavery was protected by the Constitution granting each state two senators. It maintained slavery with a balance of power in Congress between "free" and "slave" states. Slave states were joined by small states, as two senators from each state served their interests as well.

The electoral college had the same purpose.

The Civil War was a dispute over slavery in the *form* of a constitutional argument over whether a state had the (constitutional) right to secede from the Union.

After the Civil War, it was not the January 1, 1863, Emancipation Proclamation that freed the slaves, but the December 18, 1865, ratification of the Thirteenth Amendment.

The Thirteenth Amendment officially and legally ended slavery, but it left two other questions unanswered:

1. How do we bring the new freedmen into the *economic mainstream*? Their answer at the time? The Fourteenth Amendment (equal protection of the law and due process); and

2. How do we *politically enfranchise* the freedmen? Their answer? The Fifteenth Amendment (legally outlawing voter discrimination).

In 1896, *Plessy v. Ferguson* was a constitutional interpretation of the Fourteenth Amendment that gave us Jim Crow—"separate but equal"—a conservative, narrow, and strict constructionist interpretation of the Constitution.

In 1954, *Brown v. Board of Education* was a different constitutional interpretation of the Fourteenth Amendment that gave us "equal protection under the law"—a broad, liberal, or "living" interpretation of the Constitution.

Out of *Brown* sprang the modern civil rights movement of the 1950s and 1960s up until today, trying to pass and implement *legislation* under the new liberal interpretation of the Fourteenth Amendment: including the 1964 Civil Rights Act (desegregating public accommodations); the 1965 Voting Rights Act (implementing nondiscrimination in voting); the 1968 Open Housing Act; affirmative action (potentially threatened by the Supreme Court); majority-minority districts; economic set-asides for minorities and women; and the reparations movement.

The Democratic Party and the civil rights movement must work to protect these successes, but now is also the time to make the transition from "civil rights" to "human and constitutional rights."

The Democratic Party and the civil rights movement must make the transition from fighting for what appears to many—it's not true, but many see it this way—as civil rights for *some* (minorities and women) to fighting for the constitutional rights of *all*. It must move from merely fighting for *legislation* to fighting for *constitutional amendments*. It must move from a political base and a political program perceived as just for minorities, women, and progressives, to a broader political base and an agenda that is—and is perceived to be—for everybody. That's what constitutional amendments are!

How do we give the Democratic Party and the civil rights community a new message and a new direction? *By fighting for education, health care, and voting as human rights!*

Both wings of the Democratic Party share the *goal* of high-quality public education and health care for all Americans. Even President Bush and the Republicans say they want "to leave no child behind." If that's the agreed upon *goal,* then we should fight for education and health care as *human rights,* and fight to put those rights in the Constitution as *new amendments.* Policy, programs, and budgets may or may not rescue every child—either now or in the future. An individual constitutional right is the *only* actual and concrete way of making sure that no child is *ever* left behind!

Again, with respect to rights, most Americans will be surprised to learn that they don't have an affirmative "right to vote" in the Constitution. Voting is a "state right"! The lack of an affirmative right to vote in the Constitution is the reason every vote wasn't counted in 2000 and George W. Bush won.

The Fifteenth, Nineteenth, and Twenty-sixth Amendments are *nondiscrimination* amendments on the basis of race, sex, and age, respectively. Support for national election reform legislation is laudatory, but it's operating without the premise that the American people have a human and constitutional right to vote. We should first establish a *premise* by granting every American citizen an individual right to vote under the Constitution. In May 2003, in the South Carolina Democratic Party debate, the Reverend Al Sharpton asked Senator Bob Graham of Florida whether he would support adding such a voting-rights amendment to the Constitution, and he said, "probably not." Senator Graham said he thought states should control the election process, which means he's a supporter of states' rights. It also means, even after the 2000 Florida election experience, he's basically a supporter of the political status quo. Therefore, the Florida catastrophe could happen again and elsewhere. Senator Graham's rationale was also wrong. He said he didn't want to *federalize* voting. But House Joint Resolution 28 would not federalize voting any more than the First Amendment federalizes free speech. *Both are individual citizenship rights.* What Senator Graham actually did was choose states' rights over individual rights.

George Bush, instead of Al Gore, is president of the United States because we didn't have an affirmative fundamental right to vote in the Constitution, not that I'm suggesting such an amendment would be partisan. I'm not, and it wouldn't be. But in Florida, in 2000 (and elsewhere), with an affirmative right to vote in the Constitution, all of the votes would have had to be counted—using a legislatively or judicially determined equal set of criteria to judge valid and invalid ballots. Second, the Republican-controlled Florida legislature could not have threatened, as they did under Florida state law, to ignore six million popular votes cast and elect their own Bush electors (assuming Bush had gotten fewer popular votes) to send to Congress for certification if they had lost *Bush v. Gore* in the Supreme Court.

There are advantages to fighting for human rights and constitutional amendments. Human rights and constitutional amendments are *nonpartisan* (they're not Democratic or Republican), they're *nonideological* (they're not liberal, moderate, or conservative), and they're *nonprogrammatic* (they don't require a particular approach or program to be realized).

Of course, all amendments are *interpreted* by the judicial system, and ultimately by the Supreme Court. The interpretation would be based on either a relatively conservative interpretation and static view of the Constitution or a more liberal interpretation and view that sees it as a living and unfinished document. For example, *Plessy v. Ferguson* interpreted the Fourteenth Amendment conservatively as "separate but equal," and *Brown* interpreted the same amendment liberally as "equal protection under the law for all." In a nation that prides itself on the idea and ideals of democracy, over time, I believe a well-written voting-rights amendment would be interpreted by judges so as to increase democracy and the democratic participation of the people in the political process.

And if we pass new voting rights, education, and health care amendments, the *next civil rights movement* will emerge fighting for legislation to implement voting, education, and health care rights.

If we fight for *rights*, our legislative programs will logically flow from our *rights* premise. Republicans fight for a *right* to Life Amendment—and their "partial birth abortion" legislation flows naturally from their *right*. Virtually every right-wing questionnaire I get before an election begins with a *right* that they believe should be in the Constitution as a new amendment—then proceeds to policies and programs. The NRA begins with the Second Amendment, and everything they support or oppose flows from their interpretation of the Second Amendment.

If you ask any member of Congress if their education, health care, or housing plan's *goal* is for *all* Americans, they will say yes. If members support a *goal* for *all Americans*—health care for all, good education for all, affordable housing for all—why shouldn't the *goal* be a *right*? Democrats should advocate for certain basic material rights—rights that we can afford and achieve as a society—the *right* to vote, the *right* to a public education of equal high quality, and the *right* to health care.

And if Republicans and Democrats don't want to make these goals a *right for all,* make them explain *who gets them, who doesn't,* and *why!* Should only those who can afford health care get it? No, I believe health care is a human right for all Americans!

Just as Republicans vote on the Flag Amendments, Right to Life Amendments, and Tax Limitation Amendments, Democrats must insist that Congress vote on a Voting Rights Amendment, an Education Amendment, and a Health Care Amendment.

And progressives must make these amendments an issue in every U.S. House, Senate, and presidential campaign in 2004—and beyond!

That's how we give Democrats and the civil rights community a new message, a new image, and a new direction. We can be the party that fights for human rights; the party that fights to put the *right* to vote, the *right* to health care, and the *right* to a high-quality public education in the Constitution as new amendments *for all Americans.*

That's how we transform the Democrats and the traditional civil rights movement. Continue to fight, yes, but not just for civil rights, fight for human rights; fight to transform the old Democratic Party and the traditional civil rights movement into a new Democratic Party and a new constitutional rights movement; fight not just to pass legislation, but to add new amendments to the Constitution.

Progressive organizations don't have to stop what they're currently fighting for. They just need to make a constitutional amendment the goal of their struggle—*and politicize it in 2004, 2006, 2008, and beyond.*

Some will argue that constitutional amendments take too long. The Twenty-seventh Amendment, regarding congressional salaries, did take 202 years to ratify. But the Twenty-sixth Amendment—providing nondiscrimination in voting for eighteen-year-olds—required only one hundred days. It all depends on the political will of the American people at any given time.

People also fight harder for what they believe are their *rights* than they do for mere *programs.*

And, in a democratic society, rights are what the people say they are.

If Democrats and the civil rights community fight to make voting an individual citizenship right in the Constitution, the politically disenfranchised will come running.

If Democrats and the civil rights community fight to make an education of equal high quality a right in the Constitution, those families needing a better educational opportunity will come running.

If Democrats and the civil rights community fight to put health care of equal high quality in the Constitution as a right, those in need of health care will come running.

Democrats, civil rights organizations, and leaders! Fight for human rights. Fight for constitutional amendments—and the people will come running. They will follow us, and they will vote for us in record numbers!

Renewing the Democratic Party: A New Patriotism for America

Senator John Kerry

JOHN KERRY *is a United States senator from Massachusetts and Democratic candidate for president of the United States. In Vietnam, Kerry served as skipper of a Navy Swift Boat on the Mekong Delta and was awarded a Silver Star, Bronze Star, and three Purple Hearts. Upon his return home, he spoke out against the war, asking the Senate Foreign Relations Committee, "How do you ask a man to be the last man to die for a mistake?" A former prosecutor, Kerry is one of the Senate's leading national security voices and the author of a 1997 book on global crime and terrorism,* The New War.

ONE OF THE BEDROCK PROMISES OF OUR DEMOCRACY IS THE OP-portunity to prove that our faith and confidence in the future are not misplaced—or that we can turn our frustration and impatience with the present into an energy for change and a movement for reform.

I was inspired to get involved as a college student when leaders dared to challenge us to reach for our nation's highest aspirations—equality, freedom, justice. We were challenged to serve—in the Peace Corps, in our hometowns, in neighborhoods across the country, in the military, and even in our nation's capital. We responded—and we made a difference.

But my own politics were forever cemented in tougher times—the years after I came home from Vietnam. Those were years that tested our idealism. There were George Wallace and Richard Nixon—a Southern strategy—a secret plan to end the war and a secret war in Cambodia—and day by day more and more Americans drafted out of the poor rural communities and inner cities were coming home in wheelchairs and body bags. It made many of us angry—but it also made us believe that if we knocked on enough doors and raised our voices things could be different. Again a generation responded—and again a generation proved that with conviction and commitment a whole set of choices too long ignored by politicians in Washington could be put before our nation as voting issues. We proved that the politics of our nation could again respond to people's hopes for their country.

Now more than ever it's time we made that promise real for a new generation of Americans. We may be divided in this country in the votes that are cast—and divided even more so by votes never cast because too many citizens believe they can't make a difference—but that is a failure of politicians, not of our political system itself. Americans are not divided in our priorities—they deserve leaders willing to fight for those priorities with clarity and conviction. Together we can build a new politics based on common sense, accountability, and truth.

That is our obligation to our country and to ourselves—not to go along, but to set out on the path of change—for an America equal to our best possibilities and hopes. Our mission is to change politics in this country and the direction of this nation.

We must begin by telling the truth: one of the reasons so many Americans aren't interested in politics is that they think politicians aren't saying anything very interesting. The biggest threat to our party is not from our opponents, but from the growing ranks of voters who have stopped listening to either side. We must reach out to the politically homeless and give them a home again in their own democracy. People don't want a war of words; they want a contest of ideas—with action and results. Make no mistake: real leaders aren't content to win elections in which most of our fellow citizens don't want to vote.

We must have the courage of our convictions. We must be ready to refuse the course of least resistance, to confront the seemingly popular, and to offer a vision that looks beyond the next poll to the next decade and the next generation. Instead of just quoting the words of Franklin Roosevelt and John Kennedy and Robert Kennedy, we need to match their leadership with our own, with daring and commitment, with new thinking equal to a new and different time. I know the one thing America doesn't need is a second Republican Party—America needs a Democratic Party that knows what's really worth fighting for.

We must begin by demanding a different, better, fairer economic policy that grows jobs and creates wealth for all Americans. We must say it plainly: stop the new Bush tax cuts for those at the top and instead relieve the growing burden for those in the middle. Stop turning record surpluses into a new river of deficits. Stop shortchanging education, health care, and even national security to satisfy the demands of special interests at the expense of both prosperity and social progress.

We must put a whole set of choices too long deferred back on our national agenda: building housing and renewing community; guaranteeing a world-class education for every one of our kids and lifetime learning for all Americans; keeping our promise to veterans and delivering retirement security for the next generation; cleaning up our lakes and rivers and escaping the stranglehold of foreign oil by inventing our own way to energy independence; offering a new vision of tolerance and inclusiveness that respects the rights of all Americans, asks more of each of us, and helps empower the next generation of women and minority entrepreneurs; and once again asking every American to give something back to our country.

It is time to demand a different, better foreign policy—one that enlists our allies instead of alienating them and that relies on the strength of our ideals as well as our arms—a foreign policy that honors vigorous and honest debate instead of discrediting it. We must be willing to disarm weapons of mass destruction; but we must also seek to end the threat of mass starvation and disease, to stay the course of democracy and human rights, to be tough on terrorism, and equally tough on the causes of terrorism and instability. We must do this not just because it is right but because it's essential to our national security. There is nothing smart or strong or patriotic about a new unilateralism that forgets that energetic global leadership is a strategic imperative for America, not a favor we do for other countries. Leading the world's most advanced democracies isn't mushy multilateralism—it amplifies America's voice and extends our reach. Working through global institutions doesn't tie our hands—it invests U.S. aims with greater legitimacy and dampens the fear and resentment that our preponderant power sometimes inspires in others.

We can do better than we are doing today. And those who seek to lead have a duty to offer a clear vision of how we make Americans safer and make America more trusted and respected in the world. That vision is defined by looking to our best traditions—to the tough-minded strategy of international engagement and leadership forged by Wilson and Roosevelt in two world wars and championed by Truman and Kennedy in the cold war. These leaders recognized that America's safety depends on energetic leadership to rally the forces of freedom. And they understood that to make the world safe for democracy and individual liberty, we needed to build international institutions dedicated to establishing the rule of law over the law of the jungle. They spoke out for an America strong because of its ideals as well as its weapons.

For us today, the past is prologue. The same principles and strength of purpose must guide our way. Our task now is to update that tradition, to forge a bold progressive internationalism for the global age—and for Democrats to win America's confidence we must first convince Americans we will keep them safe. You can't do that by avoiding the subjects of national security, foreign policy, and military preparedness. Americans deserve better than a false choice between force without diplomacy and diplomacy without force. I believe they deserve a principled diplomacy backed by undoubted military might, based on enlightened self-interest, not the zero-sum logic of power politics, a diplomacy that commits America to lead the world toward liberty and prosperity: a bold, progressive internationalism that focuses not just on the immediate and the imminent but insidious dangers that can mount over the next years and decades, dangers that span the spectrum from the denial of democracy to destructive weapons, endemic poverty, and epidemic disease. These are, in the truest sense, not just issues of international order and security, but vital issues of our own national security.

The presidency has three key job descriptions: chief executive of the fiscal and domestic policies of the United States; head of state and therefore the nation's chief diplomat; and commander in chief of the nation's military forces. We dare not say we offer leadership and then avoid discussing two-thirds of the job; we must present a bold agenda that offers truth and vision to all Americans.

That is true not just in our foreign policy, but in our agenda right here at home. We need to again become a party that understands what it means to be progressive: forward-looking, committed to change and reform.

We are more than a party committed to any proposition

that polls at 51 percent—a party with no memory of the past and no vision of the future. We must regain the proud mantle of progressivism—the powerful claim to dynamism, proof that we understand the future potential of our country and are determined to marshal our resources to help our fellow citizens achieve and even exceed that potential.

We can't be content to be balkanized by conventional ideological formulas cooked up in Washington that matter little to Americans who want politics to speak to what really matters in their lives. Those on the alienated Left are right in saying we need bigger and bolder goals for our party and our country—a radical reduction in poverty, universal access to health care, a political system not controlled by money, an end to discrimination in any form, a global vision that embraces the possibility of peace, freedom, and prosperity in every country. Those in the disaffected Center are right in saying that results, not just dollars appropriated by government, are the best measurement of progressivism. We cannot afford to talk past each other.

Instead, we must again reach for a politics of national purpose. We must never buy into the conventional wisdom that issues are divided into those that belong to the Republicans and those that belong to us. It's defeatist for Democrats to surrender issues to Republicans without a fight. If we stay true to who we are and what we believe, we will do what the Republicans long ago stopped doing—we will reach out to our fellow Americans as citizens of the United States, not just as consumers of government benefits or tax cuts.

I've never met any Democrats active in politics who weren't

convinced they could actually do something that would benefit all of the American people and provide their children with a better future. Our whole purpose is to convince people to think beyond narrow interests and accept the responsibilities of citizenship, and the mission of spreading freedom and democracy. Why would we ever be content to look like we just want to compete with Republicans in a bidding war to convince citizens to conduct a personal cost-benefit analysis of their relationship with government and to view elections as a chance to cut a better deal?

Today's Republican strategy is to encourage Americans to ask, "What's in it for me?" Our challenge is to put our message where our heart is: asking the American people to join us in a citizens' campaign to make this country as strong, as prosperous, as wise, and as bighearted as we know we can be. On every issue, we should challenge Americans to ask themselves, "What's in it for us?"

We should ask Americans to think of the federal budget not just as a dispenser of benefits or a confiscator of wealth, but as choices we as a people have decided are important enough to sacrifice to make.

We should ask Americans to think of our foreign policy not just as a projection of our influence and our military power, but of our values and our freedoms.

We should ask Americans to declare energy independence not just because of pump prices and legroom, but because it will determine our ability to maintain our freedom and security around the world, and our ability to sustain economic growth while preserving our environment at home.

We should ask Americans to think of our civil rights not as something to be defended when it is convenient and ignored when it is not, but as fundamental to who we are to friends and enemies alike.

We should ask Americans to remember that service to country isn't something that only a few good-hearted citizens should volunteer to perform in times of peace nor should it be what those who couldn't afford to avoid it perform during times of war—it's a shared responsibility that belongs to all Americans.

The truth is, we are a generation of Democrats who learned from our parents and grandparents—and even in our own lives—what our party should always remember: that Americans are united by bonds bigger than partisanship, more important than where we live or whether we speak with an accent.

Those lessons were seared into me more than three decades ago among a special band of brothers who taught me everything I could ever want to know about our country—they were brave citizen soldiers who left behind high school and college and girlfriends and young wives to fight for their country. We grew up together on that tiny boat with a quarter-inch aluminum hull. It was where we confronted and conquered fear. It was our home away from home—our confessional—our place of silent prayer. Our boat was our sanctuary—and a place for crossing divides between Montana, Michigan, Arkansas, and Massachusetts. We never looked on one another as officer or enlisted, Okie or Down-Easter. We were just plain brothers in combat, proud Americans who together with our proud vessels answered the call. We were bound together, giving ourselves to something bigger than each and every one of us individually.

Our identity changed. When people looked at us or defined us, we were no longer the kid from South Carolina or the kid from South Boston. We were Americans. Together. All of us the same under the same flag. We learned to measure what's important through the promises we made to one another.

Those are the lessons worth living by today—and if we Democrats want to lead in America, those are the lessons that must once again guide our party.

The Dream Scenario

Senator Joe Lieberman

SENATOR JOE LIEBERMAN *(D-CT), the Democratic nominee for vice president in 2000, is currently a candidate for the Democratic nomination for president in 2004. From 1995 to 2000, he served as chairman of the Democratic Leadership Council.*

IN THE WAKE OF 2002'S ELECTIONS, WE DEMOCRATS FIND OUR-selves sailing through stormy seas—and, in many people's minds, without a compass. Some in our party believe that Democrats need to tack left to catch the growing gusts of discontent with President Bush's bad policies. Others argue that the party should lean farther to the right with the hope of riding the rising tide of moderates and independents.

But I believe this discussion misses the point. The future of our party does not rest on posturing and positioning. It's a question of principles—and just as important, ideas for realizing them. We must convince the American people that we have a vision for where we want to take the country, for meeting the specific challenges of our time, and a progressive, innovative, and unifying agenda for getting us there.

Does this mean that the Democratic Party needs a makeover? Should we simply rely on what the latest polls and focus groups tell us? Absolutely not.

The way forward for our party rests in recapturing the positive, persuasive, and principled course set by our great Democratic presidents—Roosevelt, Truman, Kennedy, Johnson, and Clinton. Each of these leaders enjoyed success at the polls because they reinvigorated our party's—and our nation's—core values for changing times. That is what we must do today.

The Democratic Party is the party of the American Dream. We believe that every person born on our soil or arriving at our shores who works hard and plays by the rules should be able to go as far as their God-given talent takes them. We believe that each one of us has a responsibility to one another and to our nation. We believe in a national community, rich in diversity and united around our shared values and aspirations. We believe in an America that is an arsenal for democracy and a beacon for freedom the world over.

Putting these values into action has produced some of the

greatest leaps in progress our nation has ever seen: the minimum wage and collective bargaining rights, Social Security and Medicare, the defeat of fascism and the building of an alliance to stand up to communism, laws to protect our air and water, the long overdue expansion of civil rights, and the historic and far-reaching prosperity of the 1990s.

Once again, the Democratic Party must update its timeless commitments to meet the new challenges we face. Specifically, we must demonstrate to the American people that we are ready, willing, and able to protect America's security, expand equal opportunity, and honor the shared values that unite us as a nation and animate our spirit as a people. When we do this, I have no doubt that Democrats will win up and down the ballot and all over the country.

Without Security, Nothing Else Matters

After September 11, our single most important responsibility is living up to our constitutional obligations to provide for the common defense and secure the blessings of liberty to ourselves and our children. The Democratic Party at its best has made America safe and strong as well as strengthened democracies and spread freedom the world over.

Moving forward, we must swiftly and aggressively transform our military to keep America safe from the new threats of tyrants and terrorists, and when it is needed, we must be prepared to use our military might to protect our security and advance our values.

At the same time, we must understand that even though America has built the most powerful fighting force in the history of the world, it is not enough to keep us safe. Too often, the Bush administration undermines our international standing when it resorts to unilateralist, often arrogant, treatment of our friends. We Democrats must insist on a foreign policy that deals more constructively and cooperatively with the other nations of the world.

Also, the war against terrorism cannot be fought with swords alone; we must use ploughshares, too. The Muslim world from which Al Qaeda emerges is in the midst of a civil war between a moderate majority, which seeks a better life, and a militant minority, which seeks to wage permanent war against all who are different. For Americans to be fully secure, we must support the moderate Muslim majority's interests and aspirations. On top of draining the terrorist swamp, we must also seed the garden—helping average men and women flourish by increasing economic opportunities and laying the institutional foundations of a civil society.

Two generations after President Roosevelt defined the Four Freedoms—freedom of expression, freedom of worship, freedom from want, and freedom from fear—too much of the world remains unfree, in desperate want, and fearful for its safety and its future. As these freedoms spread, so will our security grow.

Equal Opportunity for All

While we defend our people and stand up for democracy and freedom around the world, inside our borders we must advance the single greatest blessing of America: the promise of equal opportunity.

I have been blessed to live the American Dream. My father worked his way up from unloading the back of a bakery truck to owning his own store. My parents worked long days and too many nights to send me, the first in the family, to college.

President Bush's economic strategy—or more aptly, his lack of one—is putting the American Dream in jeopardy. I have no problem with tax cuts—but the president's tax cuts are unfair, unaffordable, and, worst of all, ineffective. Instead of jump-starting our economy and creating jobs, President Bush's policies have helped to add millions of Americans to the unemployment rolls; created the worst climate for business investment in fifty years; and dug growing deficits that are mortgaging our children's future and making it harder to meet our commitments—from homeland security to Social Security.

It is the responsibility of Democrats to offer another way— a pro-growth, progressive economic plan that revives innovation, encourages business investment, restores investor confidence, and spurs consumer spending. We did it in the 1990s, unleashing the creativity of the American people, and we can do it again today.

Strengthening Our Shared Values

Finally, we must never forget that values are what lie at the heart of politics. Politics is about choices, and the choices we make come down to what we believe is right and what we believe is wrong.

Here, we must be honest with ourselves: our party has been

uncomfortable talking about values. Too often, we've been reluctant to draw clear lines between what is right and what is wrong. And too often, we have been slow to recognize that for many Americans, understanding what's right and what's wrong flows from their faith. We must remember that faith has been a powerful ally of progress throughout American history—inspiring our Founders, the abolitionists, the suffragists, and those who marched for civil rights in our own time.

With this as our history, we must not be timid in challenging the Republican Party and its perceived monopoly on moral values. After all, this is a party that rolls back environmental protections. This is a party that is running up a national debt that our children and grandchildren will have to pay. This is a party that is more concerned with power, privilege, and partisanship than the interests of hardworking families. And it is a party that wants to use our courts to push an agenda that will turn back the clock on the gains we've made in making our country fairer and freer.

The result is an America where our differences are heightened and divisions are exploited, holding our nation back from the greatness it can achieve.

To build a national community, we Democrats must talk about—and act on—the common values that all Americans share: values like freedom, family, faith; patriotism, hard work, tolerance; opportunity for all, and responsibility from all. We must show that we are willing to put petty partisanship aside when it is for the good of the nation, and that we are equally willing to stand up for what's right for the American people.

By demonstrating that our party is committed to keeping America safe, expanding opportunity to all, and standing up for our shared values, Democrats will be honoring our party's most important principles and our most enduring legacy. More than that, I believe that this course will guide us toward political victories on Election Day and bring our entire nation closer to its inherent promise.

The Agenda of
a Republican Majority

Frank Luntz

FRANK LUNTZ *was the pollster of record for the Contract with America, the national Republican campaign effort widely credited with giving the GOP a majority in Congress in 1994 for the first time in forty years. His clients include New York City mayors Rudy Giuliani and Michael Bloomberg, as well as more than a dozen Fortune 100 companies. He has written, supervised, and conducted more than six hundred surveys, focus groups, and Instant Response sessions for corporate, media, and public affairs clients in thirteen countries since forming his company in 1992. He was a primary night and election-night commentator for* The News *with Brian Williams on MSNBC in 2000, and his "100*

Days, 1,000 Voices" segments won the coveted Emmy Award in 2001. He received his doctorate in politics at the age of twenty-five from Oxford University and served as a Fellow at Harvard University's Institute of Politics, the second youngest individual ever to receive this honor.

DEFLATE THE BALLOONS. PUT THE CORKS BACK IN THE BOTTLES. For Republicans, winning back control of the Senate and expanding their majority in the House in an economic climate of anxiety and world climate of uncertainty was quite a feat and worthy of celebration.

It shouldn't have happened. Shrinking wallets and pocketbooks had always overruled safety and security in off-year elections—until now. Midterms were always a vehicle to send "a message" to the sitting president—until now.

The lack of accurate exit polling briefly obscured a political fact now abundantly clear. First, the Democrats lost their voice. Then they lost their support. To credit President Bush for the sweeping GOP success is to miss or ignore the disintegration of the Democratic Party on all levels. Losing control of the Senate, dropping seats in the House, failing to pick up a majority of governorships, and falling to a fifty-year low in state legislative seats—it was not just a Republican success. It was a Democratic disaster.

Yes, the results of Election Day 2002 were almost as surprising as those of 1994, but in a world of four-hour news cycles, that's already ancient history. With a Republican lock on power comes a heightened level of public expectation that they may not be ready to shoulder. Hubris was the single biggest mistake of the

Republican class of 1994. When words like *landslide* and *mandate* are thrown around by some Republicans like baseballs during batting practice, one wonders whether history is about to repeat itself.

It's time for the Republicans to govern. And govern they must.

In these uncertain times, people are no longer content to subsist on the sound bites, sloganeering, and other stratagems of political gamesmanship. For a country engaged in war and not that far away from economic meltdown, no excuses for inaction will be accepted. In the words of the most famous product advertising campaign of the 1990s, just do it—and do it now.

Since 9/11, there has been a sea change in the mind-set of America. As a focus group moderator, I hear a very different voice of a very changed America. In the span of that single horrifying morning, we have come to realize that America is no longer an island unto itself, that we can no longer shut out the concerns of people who live thousand of miles apart and oceans away. More than three thousand people died that day, but the entire country was wounded and we are still overwhelmed with a feeling of vulnerability.

And while our physical security may have been the first thing we doubted in the face of a shadowy threat, our new anxiety is not so narrowly defined.

In fact, while Iraq and national security may dominate the news coverage, an underlying anxiety and economic *in*security are actually what dominates the American mind-set today. No, it is not "the economy, stupid" of Clinton and Carville. When Americans express concern about the economy today, they are really talking about their own deteriorating financial situation, the security of their very way of life. More than a third of the country has watched its personal savings and retirement nest eggs depreciate significantly, and they want that money back soon.

It is a political imperative for Republicans to pass legislation that restores confidence in the financial markets, and permanent tax relief is an essential component of financial security. True, only the most partisan Republican pollster would claim that a tax cut ranks as the number one priority in America today, but only the most partisan Democrat would be so foolish as to advocate repealing the tax cuts in these days of economic uncertainty. From income tax reductions to death tax repeal, passing a permanent tax relief package will be celebrated in Republican circles and appreciated by all taxpayers. And since most Democrats are unlikely to go along, this represents an effective way to differentiate.

The other issue that keeps cropping up is the national debt. We all remember the billboard debt counters of the late 1980s and the publicity they generated, but the American public still sees deficit reduction as secondary to economic vitality and ending wasteful Washington spending.

Individually, Americans believe that their personal economic success often necessitates taking on some debt—from home mortgages to loans for a small business. At the national level, Americans are still fed up with Washington money—*their* money—ill spent by some faceless faraway bureaucrat. As long as Republicans make a show of cutting waste, fraud, and abuse, they will be forgiven for a little red ink. But if they become obsessed with balancing books at the expense of forward economic progress, they will pay a heavy price in 2004.

Looming above and beyond the economy is the restoration of national security. Voters warmed to the Republican argument this fall that Americans cannot achieve economic, financial, or retirement security until we achieve homeland security, and they grew impatient with all the rancorous partisanship surrounding the homeland security legislation. There is a commonsense consensus across the country that we cannot regrow our economy if there are wolves gathering at the edges of, or even in, our fields.

The final component of a politically viable agenda contains a prescription drug benefit for seniors and the restoration of health security. The significance of Republicans leading the way to passage of a prescription drug benefit and reform of Medicare cannot be overstated. It could guarantee them control of Washington for multiple election cycles.

But issues and a successful legislative agenda will not guarantee Republican success in 2004.

Perceptions matter. Both parties have to cater to their powerful ideological bases, but in this worried time, the American public is demonstrating a less-than-usual tolerance for special interests or ideological jihad. What must be front and center is the business of the day, America's *security:* homeland security, international security, financial security, and *personal* security. And the party that demonstrates itself as moving toward these imperatives with greatest speed and directness will achieve the greatest electoral reward.

There are three key communication lessons from 2002 that must be learned and relearned every day.

First, overt partisanship is dead. Congressional Democratic leaders celebrated their partisanship the way a sixteen-year-old celebrates getting his driver's license—and they were duly punished. One cannot help but ponder whether a less overtly partisan celebration of the life and legacy of Paul Wellstone would have led to a different electoral outcome, or whether the attacks on President Bush delivered from Baghdad by two House Democratic leaders cost their party precious votes a few weeks later. What is clear is that the excesses of rhetoric and the deficiencies of civility did not and do not sit well with the American people. Republicans have to be careful not to engage in similar behavior.

Second, the single most important attribute of a politician today is "to say what you mean and mean what you say." It is paramount that Republicans articulate their vision and goals for the next two years in the plain speak of the average American and then go out and get it done.

And third, the party in power is expected to frame the legislative debate and educate the electorate. This year, the Democrats made a fatal mistake by perfecting the role of critic without offering a positive alternative. Next year, the Republicans need to tell the American people what they are for instead of what they are against.

On Election Night, old paradigms were broken, historic assumptions shattered. But in politics, two years is a lifetime. Today the Republicans have the wind at their back and the world at their feet. But like the weather in New England, the political winds can shift without notice.

The Mandate Bush Didn't Receive

Kate Michelman

For more than eighteen years, KATE MICHELMAN has served as president of NARAL Pro-Choice America, catapulting the organization to prominence as the nation's premier reproductive rights group. Under Kate's leadership, NARAL Pro-Choice America has transformed the political debate and positioned a woman's freedom to choose as a fundamental American liberty.

THE 2002 MIDTERM ELECTIONS MUST BE ACKNOWLEDGED FOR what they were: a political victory for President Bush. It is just as important that they be understood for what they were *not*: an endorsement of the extreme social agenda, especially assaults on reproductive rights. Beneath that fact lays this irony: Republicans successfully commandeered the rhetoric of defending freedom against threats from overseas but are now using that success to attack freedom for half the population—American women—at home.

The right to the full range of reproductive choices—from preventing unwanted pregnancy to bearing healthy children to choosing legal abortion—is an essential part of a century of steady progress toward freedom and equality for women. The ability to control the timing and circumstances of pregnancy is integral to women's health, their children's welfare, and, above all, to freedom itself. Our challenge, as the critical elections of 2004 approach, is to defend freedom of choice as a core value rather than a caricature. To be pro-choice is to believe that human beings are distinguished from other species by the ability to exert moral judgment on the situations that shape our lives rather than being powerless captives of circumstance. Neither should we yield the territory of spiritual belief. The God anti-choice politicians invoke to attack reproductive liberty is the same God that endowed individuals with moral judgment and free will.

While we must defend legal abortion vigorously, we cannot limit ourselves to a defensive posture or we risk being marginalized as simply the vocal opponents of a popular president. Instead, we must pursue a proud, pro-active agenda that equips every woman with the tools—including access to sexuality education, contraception, legal abortion, and prenatal care—to exercise her free will in accordance with her own values. This agenda must prepare us to defend freedom of choice regardless of whether *Roe v. Wade* survives the intense assault it now faces. Its centerpiece must be an all-out effort to motivate and mobilize a pro-choice majority in the United States.

Polling consistently shows that Americans embrace the right to choose when they recognize the threats it faces and are offered a positive value to embrace. Research just as consistently indicates that Republicans do not have the anti-choice mandate they now claim. Reproductive freedom may be among the first casualties of the 2002 elections, but it was hardly the primary issue on voters' minds. Anti-choice candidates clearly know this, as most sought to conceal their anti-choice views. The most significant Republican victories—those in Senate campaigns—occurred because President Bush succeeded in nationalizing the election on issues like homeland security. But in races where more particular concerns played out—especially gubernatorial campaigns—freedom of choice was decisive for several candidates, including pro-choice governors in Illinois, Kansas, Michigan, New Mexico, Pennsylvania, and Wyoming.

Still, Republican leaders on Capitol Hill almost immediately announced plans to pursue an aggressive social conservative agenda, with legal abortion and reproductive rights squarely in the center of the legislative bull's-eye. The White House expressed trepidation about that strategy, but the president's concern, it must be understood, was a matter of politics, not principle: his objection was not that Republican leaders *will* pursue that agenda, but that they *said* they would do so. From its first day in office, the Bush administration has attempted to conceal the intensity of its anti-choice views behind moderate rhetoric. The administration repeatedly claimed that President Bush's deep-seated opposition to freedom of choice was irrelevant because, as a matter of practical politics, Congress would never act on the issue. Now that claim has been exposed as hollow.

The Republican Congress will continue to press for a variety of measures steadily eroding a woman's freedom to choose—bills that will have a lasting impact regardless of whether *Roe v. Wade* stands. Those bills confront President Bush with real, not hypothetical, choices, and it strains credibility to believe that he will do anything other than sign them into law.

Nor is the White House in a solely reactive posture on the issue. President Bush has already launched a full-scale campaign to pack the federal courts with judges hostile to *Roe*. If a single Supreme Court vacancy occurs, he could have the opportunity to nominate—and the Senate would undoubtedly confirm—the one anti-choice justice whose vote could severely eviscerate *Roe's* protections.

It is critical that pro-choice Americans forestall that possibility for the remainder of President Bush's current term. But if he is reelected—and especially if the anti-choice Senate survives along with him—it will become highly difficult, if not impossible, to preserve *Roe*. The pro-choice movement will be forced to reestablish reproductive freedom as a constitutional right, a process that took decades the first time and could take just as long if it must be repeated. We should not cling to illusions about what that means. If *Roe* falls, fully half the states will likely ban or further restrict legal abortion. Women will die in back alleys. Others will be forced to bear children against their will, with terrible consequences for everyone involved.

And a ban on abortion will be just a beginning for anti-choice politicians. The same legal reasoning they employ to attack

Roe could also be used to undermine landmark Supreme Court decisions guaranteeing the right to birth control. And ultimately, the anti-choice movement sees *Roe* as a symbol of the progress women have made in achieving equality in American society. One leading anti-choice spokesman recently said his movement's goal was to return to a pre-1973 America. That includes a ban on abortion, but we dare not ignore the unspoken objective: a society where women are unwelcome in any role other than their biological function of bearing children.

If that vision seems ominous, it is. But it is a recitation of cold fact, not a hypothesis of what may occur. And there is positive news as well: when Americans know that freedom of choice is gravely and palpably threatened, they are motivated to vote on that basis. The pro-choice movement and pro-choice candidates must make the right to choose a defining issue in the 2004 elections. NARAL Pro-Choice America has launched a full-scale mobilization to educate Americans about threats to freedom of choice and motivate them to vote their pro-choice beliefs.

Justice Harry Blackmun, who authored the decision in *Roe v. Wade*, once wrote of the freedom to choose: "I fear for the future. . . . The signs are evident and a chill wind blows." After the 2002 elections, that wind is howling at gale force. If we are to survive the storm and prevail in 2004, pro-choice Americans must reclaim the mantle of freedom. The only way to save freedom of choice is the same means by which Americans have preserved other fundamental freedoms throughout our history: by mobilizing and fighting. We intend to do precisely that.

Redefining the Center Right

Georgette Mosbacher

GEORGETTE MOSBACHER *is the chief executive officer of Bor-*
ghese, Inc. She is the author of two books, Feminine Force *and* It
Takes Money, Honey, *and is the founder of the Children's Advo-*
cacy Center of Manhattan. She is a trustee for National Realty
Trust and holds a membership on the boards of the Hudson River
Park Trust and the USO of Metropolitan New York. She is also
the Republican national committeewoman for the state of New
York.

THE RESULTS OF THE 2002 GENERAL ELECTION WILL BE STUDIED
for years to come by historians and journalists, but one thing was

instantly clear the moment the polls closed: the split decision of the 2000 election was a distant memory. When the ballots were tallied, it became obvious that voters had made a distinct choice in favor of the Republican Party. President George W. Bush had campaigned hard for candidates of his party, and the investment paid off. The GOP expanded its majority in the House of Representatives and regained control of the Senate. For the first time in U.S. history, the president's party *gained* seats in the House during the administration's first midterm elections, and the same history-making turn was achieved in the Senate. In a major vote of confidence, the American people handed their Republican president majority control of both houses of the legislature.

How did it happen? The answers can be found in three trends that began long before November 5, 2002: the emergence of the baby boomers as a formidable—and increasingly conservative— force in American politics, a major redefinition of the political center to the right, and a renewal of faith as a touchstone in American life.

In 1994, the first wave of baby boomers began to turn fifty years old. The midterm election held that year produced stunning results; with a Democrat in the White House, the Republican Party took control of the House of Representatives and a majority of the statehouses for the first time in decades. This was due largely to the growing conservatism of the baby boomers, the largest demographic group and biggest voting bloc in the United States. As they began to reach retirement age, many boomers began to reassess their political values. As their lives changed— children leaving the nest, retirement approaching—so did their political orientation. Liberal philosophies of their past were replaced with an ever-increasing concern over retirement savings, a punitive tax system, a failing Social Security system, education reform, and health care—for themselves, their grown children, grandchildren, and elderly parents.

Boomers' changing priorities resulted in a major political realignment rightward, begun in 1994 and reaffirmed in 2002. Boomers are a goal-oriented, problem-solving group. They do not want to hear endless political debate or criticism without being offered sound solutions. In 1994, the Republicans put forth the Contract with America, which tackled some of the most vexing national problems by delivering results such as tax cuts, crime reduction, and welfare reform.

Coming to power in 1994 along with the GOP Congress were thirty-two Republican governors, who represented a new wave of problem solving. At the state level, these governors also delivered innovative solutions: they showed that taxes could be cut and state economies stimulated without sacrificing services, invigorated entrepreneurship could result in significant job creation, crime could be reduced by double-digit percentages, and welfare reform could result in major reductions of the welfare rolls.

The Republican Congress in 1994 and the Republican governors of that era took control of traditionally Democratic issues and applied conservative solutions. The results were dramatic, and the Republicans continued to press their agenda, despite the obstacles involved with having to work with a Democratic president. When voters saw that Republicans were producing results, at both the state and national levels, they responded at the voting booth.

President Bush understood this dynamic better than many of his contemporaries. He spoke to the issues about which boomers cared and offered bold and innovative solutions based on the successes of the 1994 class of Congress and governors: income tax, capital gains, and dividend tax relief; school vouchers; faith-based initiatives. The agenda built creatively and boldly on the first wave of Republican policy triumphs that came in the mid-1990s.

While the Republicans were adapting and succeeding, the Democrats remained focused on themes that had worked for them thirty years before but no longer had resonance.

On taxes, for example, the Democrats trotted out their shopworn argument about tax cuts favoring the rich. That kind of class warfare worked wonders for them when only a small percentage of the very wealthiest Americans owned stocks and bonds. But today, when over 60 percent of Americans own stock in some form, those old Democratic approaches failed.

The Democrats were asleep when Main Street bought into Wall Street. Most boomers hold stocks and bonds. Class divisions do not exist as sharply as they did in the past. While the Democrats were still campaigning in the politics of yesterday, talking in antiquated terms about "the rich," the Republicans had already moved on, led by a president who looked his fellow boomers in the eye and offered new solutions. When Bush was first elected, he delivered on his promise to cut marginal income tax rates; when the 2002 election arrived, *voters knew he meant what he said on taxes*. When the Democrats bellyached about a capital gains tax cut benefiting the rich, many boomers rolled their eyes and voted Republican: owning stock didn't make boomers rich, necessarily;

it made them shareholders who deserved a tax break in an over-taxed society.

The Democrats also stayed closely allied with the trade unions, which undercut their ability to appeal to boomers and others—voters who relied less on the unions and more on corporate guarantees, such as 401(k) plans. More and more voters realized that union demands often made their companies less competitive and profitable, which, in turn, hurt their job security. There was a growing sense among traditionally Democratic union voters that business was no longer the *enemy* but the *employer* that provided the 401(k), the pension, and the health benefits. Now invested in their companies, many voters no longer responded to the Democrats' demonization of business.

The Republicans also benefited from another major shift in mainstream and Main Street America: increased comfort with their own and others' spirituality. September 11, 2001, changed everything: international politics, domestic politics and policy, and the president and his administration. It changed the way the American people view threats to U.S. security and the nature of evil in the world. It also made most Americans more introspective as they reexamined their faith. This, in turn, had a dramatic effect on how the president's strong faith was perceived; many who had previously been threatened by his personal faith in God came to accept it. As they turned to a Higher Being for comfort and answers, they became increasingly comfortable with a president who did the same. Instead of being resentful or fearful or dismissive of his faith, they trusted it. And they trusted him because of it.

The titanic new wave of patriotism and spirituality brought

about by September 11 reaffirmed the basic conservative values of God and country. The center was redefined rightward once again, and once again the Democrats missed it. When the president summed up September 11 in one four-letter word, *evil,* voters got the biblical meaning behind it. They didn't criticize it out of fear or political correctness. Instead, they embraced it. Several months later, a liberal group backed a drive to remove the words *under God* from the Pledge of Allegiance. The backlash was fierce: mainstream America reacted with strong support for keeping the words in the Pledge. The war on terror accelerated the shift away from liberalism, and, again, the left either didn't see it or didn't want to see it.

In 2002, the Democrats did not lose the issues to Bush and his team. The Democrats had been losing the issues all along, particularly since 1994, when the baby boom generation began to enter their fiftieth year with a new maturity and appreciation for personal responsibility and political reality. That major demographic shift had seismic political implications and the Republican Party was the first—indeed the only—party to respond and act.

The lesson of 2002, therefore, should not be lost on Republicans: voters—particularly that huge bloc of baby boomers—trust them to protect their national, individual, and economic security. If the Republicans exercise their majority power wisely and efficiently, the realignment favoring the GOP begun in 1994 and continued through 2002 could last indefinitely. And that would truly be a political revolution.

Dem Problems: A Great Political Party Can't Thrive on Snob Appeal

Peggy Noonan

PEGGY NOONAN *is the bestselling author of six books, most recently* A Heart, a Cross and a Flag, *a collection of her columns that was published in June 2003 by Simon & Schuster. She is a contributing editor of* The Wall Street Journal *and a commentator for MSNBC and NBC News. Noonan is a former special assistant to President Ronald Reagan. She lives in Brooklyn, New York.*

DEAR ANDREW,

As a former Democrat I'm happy to talk to my old party about its future. Some of my words may sting a little, but I send them to you in hopes your party will see in them food for thought, and for progress.

All political parties have problems—infighting, internal dissent, philosophical disagreements. But the modern Democratic Party has problems that are essentially different from that, and could actually do it in.

The first is what seems to me a lack of a constructive spirit within your party. Great parties exist in part to give us markers for the future. They offer a rough map that will get us to a better and higher destination. In the Democratic Party now, and for some time, I have not perceived that they are trying to get us to a good place. They seem interested only in thwarting the trek of the current president and his party, who are, to the Democrats, "the other." When the president is a Democrat you now support him no matter what. You support him if he doesn't have a map, and isn't interested in markers, and is interested only in his own day-to-day survival.

I am not saying you are too partisan. Partisanship is fine. But Republicans by and large don't suffer from blind loyalty or blind antagonism. They would think it irresponsible to the country. They will bolt on one of their own if he insists on a route they think is seriously wrong (the first Bush on taxes). They will kill his presidency if they conclude he is essentially destructive (it was his Republican base in Congress that ended Richard Nixon's career). Recently it was Republicans who did in their own Senate majority leader because they would not accept a certain kind of nonsense. If George W. Bush begins to seriously compromise conservative political philosophy, or to behave in a manner grossly offensive in a leader, they will turn on him, too.

The Democratic Party will now stick with its guy forever, no matter how harmful he is. Perhaps you call that loyalty, and perhaps there's something to it, but a bigger part, I believe, is that you have come to think that winning is everything—that victory is the purpose of politics.

If the purpose is just winning, you can do anything to win. And you can do anything to stay. You never give an inch. But people who never give an inch sometimes wind up occupying tired and barren terrain.

You have grown profoundly unserious. This is the result of the win-at-any-cost mind-set. A recent illustration: President Bush broke through to the great middle of America and persuaded them we must move in Iraq. He was able to do this not because the presidency is the Big Microphone—President Clinton used to complain that Rush Limbaugh had the big microphone—but because he honestly believed, in his head and his heart, he was acting to make our country and other countries safer. Maybe history will show him right and maybe not, but people can tell his passion springs from conviction.

Democratic leaders, on the other hand, have by and large approached Iraq not with deep head-heart integration but with what appears to be mere calculation. What will play? What will resonate? These questions are both inevitable and a part of politics. But again, they are not the purpose of politics. Lincoln himself said, "Public opinion is everything," but he was speaking of public opinion as a fact he had to consider as he tried to push the country in a new direction. He did not think public opinion itself was a direction. And he didn't think it was a policy.

The modern Democratic Party is unserious in other ways. In

the 1950s and '60s the party included many obviously earnest and thoughtful liberals who supported goals that were in line with and expressions of serious beliefs. They believed that America was an exceptional country. (See the speeches of Adlai Stevenson among others.) Because it was exceptional it needed to remain strong. (JFK: "We shall pay any price, bear any burden, meet any hardship . . . to assure the survival and the success of liberty.")

They also believed America had real flaws, actual sins, that needed to be righted. They assumed this exceptional country could right them. (That's what optimism is in politics; it's not smiling a hearty smile in front of a podium and pointing with a commanding air toward all your friends in the audience.) They wanted racial integration for the good of justice and the good of our country. They wanted more government assistance to the poor for the same reason. They were anticommunist. They were grown-ups. They were thinking. Vietnam changed everything, of course, and even though this is an old story I'll touch on it. Your party's problem was not that it opposed the war—that was one honorable position among many. The mistake the Democrats made was to allow their antiwar movement to become infused with bitterness and hostility, with a spirit of destructiveness. By the end the animating spirit of the movement looked something like this: We do not love this place; we prefer leaders unsullied by the grubby demands of electoral politics; we are drawn to the ideological purity of Ho, Fidel, Mao. And by the way we're taking over: oppose our vision and we'll take care of you by revolutionary means.

That was the ultimate spirit of the movement, and it began to take over your party. The old-bull liberals were swept away, more radical Democrats arose, and they led your party to become not a united and spirited force but a party of often warring pressure groups. The pro-abortion lobby, the affirmative-action lobby, other lobbies. You have had only one two-term Democratic president in the thirty-five years since Vietnam. This is because in the end you looked extreme, bought and paid for, and weak.

The Republican Party still manages to cohere around principles that are essentially clear and essentially conservative. The Democrats are not cohering. They are held together by a gritty talent for political process—message discipline, for instance. But what good is message discipline if there's no serious and coherent message?

There is another problem. You have become the party of snobs. You have become the party of Americans who think they're better than other Americans.

Let me quickly chart the life of a former Democrat. When I was a teenager in the 1960s, the Democrats seemed to me the party of the working class and middle class—the party of immigrants, strivers, and those who adhered to an expansive reading of the American Dream. I shared that dream, and saw my home as the Democratic Party. I was swayed by JFK and Bobby, by their implicit sense of honor about being Americans, as if they thought to be an American was a great gift and yet had a price: you had to help your country, you had to have guts and an open mind, you had to care about people others forgot.

I thought of Republicans as bland, unimaginative, vaguely immoral people who drank things like gin and tonic where they played things like golf. I remember reading in high school or college and being moved by someone's wonderful old turn-of-the-century agitprop poem—"The golf links lie so near the mill / That almost every day / The laboring children can look out / And watch the men at play." I assumed those men were Republicans.

My father had been a poor kid in Brooklyn who grew up on what was then called relief. He'd talk about the rancid butter people like him were given to eat. But he thought Franklin Roosevelt was the only president who'd ever done anything to help the workingman, and he had a resentment of those who were comfortably middle class, or upper middle, or rich. I inherited this. These were the biases I brought to the conversation when talk turned to politics when I was a teenager and young woman.

But—again—the antiwar movement startled me. I knew America was imperfect, but I also loved it. I had no illusion that other countries were perfect, or superior. I couldn't imagine an unelected dictator had more legitimacy than an American president. I will never forget a moment when on local television they showed one day an antiwar march meeting up with a bunch of New York hard hats near city hall. They fought, and the hard hats tried to raise the American flag. I watched and realized I was pulling for the hard hats.

I worked in Boston after college and saw affluent, well-educated, and deeply insensitive officials forcing busing on working-class people who were understandably aghast at the idea that their young children couldn't go to the school down the block but had to be bused to a place far away where they knew nobody. I worked in an all-news radio station, and many of my colleagues, the writers and editors and producers, were young liberals gone left, bright and engaged by life. They were almost all for busing. Their enthusiasm for it—they hadn't yet had children whose presence might have moderated their thoughts and conclusions—left them patronizing the ill-educated and no doubt racist poor-Irish-Catholics-who-have-nothing people of South Boston, who opposed busing. Again I was startled. This was like the antiwar movement. It was like Henry Cabot Lodge looking down on the help! It would never have occurred to me to look down on anyone. But boy, these liberals did. They were real snobs. And it was class snobbery.

I was, as a young woman in the '70s, trying to commit myself professionally for the first time. I wanted to do good work, and really tried. But I saw in time that I was being clobbered by taxes, and in time I had a subversive thought. Hmmm, liberals who back busing are taxing me extra heavy so I can pay for busing. Great.

Liberals were also acting as if street crime was an inevitable result of societal injustice. I didn't doubt there was truth in that, but I also knew street crime was the result of street criminals, and they should be caught and thrown in jail. But how can you find time to do that when you're busy reforming society top to bottom like little Pol Pots? In fact, why do it at all when the fact of exploding street crime seems to support your theories about American inequality and injustice?

Once one late night on the T, the city transit system, I got off at a downtown stop and noticed a woman who'd gotten off with me. She was about sixty, she was furiously going through her purse, and she had the kind of flopping expression of someone who's just lost control of her facial muscles. I asked what was wrong and she turned to me and began to cry. She said she'd had her purse next to her on the subway, she feared the kid next to her had opened it, she was afraid, she got off, and all her money was gone. He'd taken everything. She did not appear to be someone who could lose $40 or $60 lightly. I helped her report it and I think I gave her money. But hers was truly the face of the oppressed: an old lady alone who's lost control of her face. And who was oppressing her? It wasn't the tough-on-crime crowd.

All of it came together bit by bit, and I started to become a conservative, and in time a Republican. And for the very reasons that my father was a Democrat.

Not a word of what I am saying is new. You've heard stories like this before. But it is still fiercely pertinent to your fortunes, because the journey I describe was common. It was the journey millions and tens of millions of people were taking at the same time, in the same era, for the same reasons. By the '80s their numbers were massive. They were the ground troops of the Reagan revolution. They left the Democratic Party. They left you. Here's your problem: to this day they haven't come back.

And they're not teaching their kids to love you.

I see the modern Democratic Party as the party of snobs. I wonder why your much-proclaimed compassion is distributed on such a limited basis—to this pressure group, that minority group, this special-interest group.

Yes, all parties do this to some degree, but again, the Republicans the past quarter century seemed to be building coalitions that embraced the same general principles—freedom in the world, security at home, smaller and less mighty government wherever possible, more money left in the pockets of the people, a respect for the things that were tried and true. They recognize the fact of evil in the world, and they're unwilling to excuse crime and criminals.

The Democrats seemed motivated not by general principles and beliefs but only the need to win, which left you protecting your market share by bribing groups you'd once been able to champion. You've become confused as to your purpose, your reason for being. Yes, Republicans have pressure groups too, and the party pays great attention to them. But the GOP's pressure groups are in line with the sympathies of the party as a whole. When the National Rifle Association agitates for its issues, it's agitating within a party that supports the right to keep and bear arms.

Let's stick with the right to keep and bear arms for a minute. My Democratic friends, when you think about this question, ask yourself if snobbery as a political force isn't part of the reason you stand where you stand.

Gun owners hunt. They keep guns to protect themselves in dangerous places—rural areas where help isn't always immediately available, for instance. They like and respect firearms and are committed to their right to have them. A lot of gun owners live down south or out west or in the less fashionable sections of the northern industrial states. They are mostly not coastal and urban in their cultural interests. They are not the media elite, the academic elite, any kind of elite. Do you respect these people?

As long as they're law abiding, and responsible enough to respect the damage guns can do, conservatives completely support their right to have arms. (Sure they should be registered, but registration should exist to allow the law-abiding to have guns, and not be twisted into a way to keep guns out of everyone's hands.)

Liberals/leftists as a class—and I'm sorry but really, you've become a class—don't usually know people who shoot. They don't like people who shoot. They look down on them; gun owners are boobs and yahoos out in the sticks killing Bambi. As for living in a rural area where there's no nearby police force, why don't you just . . . move?

Let me be, admittedly, mean, but to make a point I can't figure out how to make any other way. Those who oppose the right to keep and bear arms are not as a rule the kind of people who would, or could, take down a nut waving his gun at the kids in a McDonald's. Those who oppose gun rights are more like the kind of people who when the incident was over would write a sensitive essay about how it felt to come face-to-face with one's existential powerlessness when faced with the sudden force of a sick man who alas shot two kids right in front of me. You may mean to be helpful in the abstract, but you are not helpful in the particular.

Conservatives are on the side of the citizen who'd protect the kids and take down the bad guy with the gun. Aren't you, really? Shouldn't you be, "for the good of the children"?

Do you wish Todd Beamer, Tom Burnett, and the stewardesses and pilots of the hijacked jets of 9/11 had been armed? I do. "That's a dramatic, worst-case scenario," you say. Sure. But life is full of dramatic, worst-case scenarios. Is your life so comfortable and protected that you've forgotten this? Did you ever know it? Really, doesn't mere snobbery have something to do with where you stand?

This is the Democratic paradox: you want so much to run America and yet you seem not so fond of Americans.

Here is a challenge for modern Democrats. The old things

the party stood for—civil rights, Social Security, Medicare, the women's movement, a more appreciative and accepting view of those who feel marginalized—have been fully or in good part achieved. And the Democrats now seem like people who've run out their string and have grasped at radicalism not only because of lingering '60s sentiment but also, simply, to stay afloat.

An example: abortion. The Democrats became the party of what they called abortion rights. Fine. It seemed to them right at the time and a step toward human progress. But now, thirty years later, after all the things we've seen and pondered, after all that science has shown us, the Democratic Party has grown not less radical on abortion, but more. Your party won't even agree to ban third-term abortions—which is the abortion of a baby who looks and seems fully human and capable of life because he is. The Democrats oppose parental consent even in the cases of fourteen-year-olds who are themselves children. It opposes directing doctors to inform frightened young women before an abortion is performed that there are other options, other possible paths.

This is so radical. So out of touch with the feeling and thought of the vast middle of the country. So at odds with our self-image as a nation. We think we try to protect the vulnerable. We think we're kind.

Democratic leaders are radical on abortion because they live in fear of—brace yourself, more snobs coming—a pro-abortion lobby that has money, clout, and workers, and that can kill the hopes of any Democratic aspirant who doesn't toe the line. And that pro-abortion lobby is largely composed of the professionals, journalists, lawyers, and operatives who long ago showed such contempt for America. And for Southie. And for taxpayers. And for those who hold to a spiritual or nonspiritual sense of right and wrong, good and evil, and who have a visceral sense that abortion is bad for our nation and its future.

The Democratic Party's complete obeisance to this lobby makes Democrats look bought, frightened, and craven. It also makes them look stone cold. You look that way when you back stone-cold policies.

Here's a funny thing. I've met a lot of the Democratic nomination hopefuls, and they don't seem cold or indifferent. They seem like people who are doing what they think they have to do to survive. You're making these guys do some bad things.

And there's this. Deep down, in some still vital area of human knowledge within you, the place where you just know things, you have got to know that no political party primarily funded, supported, and led by fierce pro-abortionists, by people whose great interest in life is seeing to it that the right to kill infants is retained, can long endure. Nothing can long stand on a foundation like that. Nothing.

One wishes the Democrats well if for no other reason than the Republican Party will be at its best only when it faces a worthy and vital competitor.

So here's my advice: Look at the clock. Know what time it is. Half the country is wondering if we are in the end times. (Excuse me, I mean they fear man may be living through a final, wrenching paroxysm, the result of man's inhumanity to man and of the inevitable culmination of several unhelpful forces and trends.) So wake up and get serious. Get your heart back, and your guts. Be constructive, not destructive. Help. If President Bush advances an agenda you deep down support, then go public and help him. If he advances what you honestly oppose, come forward with constructive alternatives.

Don't "position" yourself on issues like Iraq, think about your position on Iraq and be guided by a question: What will be good and right for America and the world? Reach your conclusions and hold to them as long as you can hold them honestly. A lot of people, not all but many, can see when you're only positioning yourselves.

Stare down the abortion lobby, the gun-ban nuts, etc. Be moderate. Make progress. The next time someone like the late Bob Casey, a popular governor of a great industrial state and pro-life due to conscience, asks to address your convention, let him. Welcome him. People like him widen the tent.

Be pro-free-speech again. Allow internal divisions and dissent. A vital political party should have divisions and dissent.

Develop a new and modern Democratic rationale—the reason regular people should be Democrats again. Stop being just the We Hate Republicans Party. That's not a belief, it's a tic.

Stop being the party of snobs. Show love for your country and its people—all its people. Stop looking down on those who resist your teachings.

Stop taking such comfort in Bill Clinton's two wins. Move on. He was a great political talent, but he won by confusing the issues, not facing them. That's a trick that tends to work only at certain times and only with powerful charisma. And even with that his leadership will be remembered, is already being remembered, as "a holiday from history," in Charles Krauthammer's phrase. And he never hit 50 percent of the vote in either of his victories, even when he had peace and riotous prosperity on his side. He didn't have coattails. (See Gore, Albert, Jr., life of.) And he rose in large measure because George H. W. Bush broke his pledge, raised taxes, and saw the economy plummet. That was calamitous for the Republicans. Your great hope now is more calamity. If George W. Bush suffers a post–9/11 disaster at home or abroad in the next few years it may—may—propel a Democrat into the White House. But who respects a party whose great hope is widespread pain?

So stop allowing Bill Clinton to present himself as Mr. Democrat. Ask him to stay home. He reminds people of embarrassment. He uses up all your oxygen. Love him or hate him, we all know he's the personification of slick, and slick isn't what you want as the face of a great party.

Stop the ideology. A lot of Democratic Party movers and intellectuals have created or inherited a leftist ideology that they try to impose on life. It doesn't spring from life; it's forced on life, and upon people. Stop doing that—it's what weirdos who are detached from reality do. Have a philosophy instead of an ideology, hold it high and dear, and attempt to apply it, not impose it.

Respect normal Americans again, even those who are not union members. We're all touched by grace, we all deserve a voice, and you could learn a few things if you'd listen to those who've had to struggle through life.

And by the way, I'd like it if you started smoking again, at least for a while. Democrats were nicer when they smoked. Then they let all those Carrie Nation types in the party beat them to a pulp, and regular Democrats stopped feeling free to be regular flawed messy humans. That was too bad. Why don't you send the smoking-ban lobby back to the abortion-rights meeting, and tell them to leave you alone?

You're still one of our two great political parties. Show some class, the good kind. Throw your cap over the wall, as JFK said, and boldly follow.

The War After the War:
The Parties Fight for Advantage
After 9/11 and Iraq

Norman Ornstein

A resident scholar at the American Enterprise Institute, NORMAN
ORNSTEIN *also serves every two years as an election analyst for*
CBS News. *He write a weekly column, "Congress Inside Out,"
for* Roll Call, *the newspaper of Capitol Hill, and is a member of
the Board of Contributors of* USA Today. *He is a senior counselor
to the Continuity of Government Commission, looking to ensure
that our governing institutions can function in the event of a terrorist attack on Washington.*

DEMOCRATS WERE DOWNCAST THE MORNING AFTER THE NOVEM-
ber 2002 midterm elections, much as they had been downcast and

distraught following the November 1994 midterm elections (in which they lost the Congress and saw Newt Gingrich emerge as the first Republican Speaker of the House in forty years). At a seminar soon after the 1994 results were in, I gave Democrats a counterintuitive and more soothing message: like Wagner's music, it is not as bad as it sounds.

With America's system of checks and balances and divided powers, controlling the reins of power is not always all it seems. Bill Clinton's first two years as president were spent with full Democratic Party control of the machinery of power in Washington, with seemingly comfortable margins in both houses of Congress. They were miserable years for him. Republicans, shut out of power for the first time in a dozen years, started with a basic message of their own to the new president—"You are on your own. Don't count on us for any assistance; get your votes from your majority Democrats."

So the president's top priority, an economic plan, was delayed for months, as he had to find majorities with only Democratic votes. He eventually succeeded, by one vote in each of the two houses, but the process of gathering the requisite votes was a difficult and humiliating one, and the delays robbed the president of any momentum or victory dance after he won—and thus of any accrual of political capital necessary to win additional policy victories. The lack of Republican votes, along with the cavalier and undisciplined attitude of Democrats in Congress who had held their majorities for decades regardless of the party of the president, meant other setbacks, on a crime bill and on the president's signature health care reform plan.

The failure of the health care plan contributed significantly to the Republican sweep in 1994. But after the Gingrich-led House Republicans passed most of their Contract with America early in 1995, their momentum slowed when the Republican Senate balked and the president got his legs back. With Clinton using Gingrich as a foil, and using the hubris of the House Republicans, like a jujitsu master, to turn their aggressiveness against them, he gained enough strength in two years to become the first Democratic president since Franklin Roosevelt to win reelection.

It was Republicans who were downcast and distraught in the spring of 2001 when Republican senator Jim Jeffords of Vermont switched to independent status and moved his institutional support to the Democrats—changing control of the Senate from Republican to Democratic in one fell swoop. Once again, the message (this time to Republicans) was Wagnerian; it is not as bad as it sounds.

To be sure, the new Democratic majority used its control of the agenda to hold hearings and frame issues in the Senate that bedeviled and enraged Republicans. But it also gave President Bush and his White House a foil. Democrats in the majority needed fifty-one votes to gain control of the agenda on the floor, to pass bills that could get to conference with the Republican-led House and force compromises. To do so often meant keeping near-perfect unity among the fifty Democrats plus Jeffords, something that often eluded Majority Leader Tom Daschle. Despite his strenuous efforts, he faced the persistent defection of Georgia's Zell Miller and frequent defection of other conservative Democrats. Division in Democratic ranks meant no unified Democratic position on key issues, allowing the president nearly full domination of the bully pulpit. Bush was thus able to go into the 2002 campaign blaming Democrats for gridlock and failure, while taking full credit for any successes.

The election result was striking. For only the third time since the Civil War, the president's party actually gained seats in the House of Representatives—the first time for a Republican president—and it broke a not inexorable but quite consistent pattern of the president's party losing seats in the U.S. Senate. For the first time in modern memory, maybe the first time ever, presidential coattails seemed to play a critical role in the unusual Republican gains in Congress. And those gains, of course, had the added impact of turning the Senate's majority from Democratic to Republican, giving President Bush unified control in Washington, a rare asset for Republican presidents over the past seventy-five years. The postelection press analysis of the election certainly treated the results as a huge and historic breakthrough for President Bush and the GOP.

The message to Democrats: it is not as bad as it sounds. For one thing, while the election results were historic, they did not signal the kind of profound shift that might mean a fundamental change in the nation's political dynamics. The Republicans gained a net of 6 seats out of 435 in the House, a net of 2 in the 100-member Senate, and lost three governorships—numbers that do not suggest a Republican trend of tidal-wave proportions.

Taking a slightly longer view, Democrats had gained seats in the House each of the three preceding national elections—and winning seats four times in a row is both difficult and rare, since the vulnerable seats, or targets of opportunity held by one's opponents, become progressively reduced in number with each gain. (On the other hand, in the Senate, where twenty of the thirty-four seats up for contest were held by Republicans, making their potential vulnerability greater, a Republican gain was indeed noteworthy.) The bottom line: the virtual parity at all levels between the two parties that had been evidenced in the 2000 results remains in place.

More important is the mixed blessing that comes with full control of the reins of power, especially when combined with narrow majorities. Democrats have lost their piece of the agenda, their staff dominance, their chairmanships. But President Bush has lost his foil; it will be much harder to blame Democrats for policy failures or gridlock. At the same time, Democratic Senate leader Tom Daschle no longer requires fifty-one votes as an ante to get his place at the policy table. Republicans in the Senate need sixty votes to overcome Democratic-led filibusters, and have to cope with the multitude of tactics in the individualistic Senate, like the hold, that can clog the agenda pipeline. Needing only to keep nine Democrats from defecting to the Republican side, Daschle no longer has to pay constant attention to Zell Miller and other conservatives. And the animosity Senate Democrats feel toward the president for his partisan efforts in the 2002 campaign ensure a solid core of opposition to many of the Bush domestic proposals, along with a skepticism toward his foreign policy.

At the same time, Republicans in Congress, with no one else to blame, will be more sensitive to public opinion and more nervous about their own accountability as the 2004 elections approach. Thus, it became evident early on in the 108th Congress that the Bush tax cut proposals would not achieve the unanimous or near-unanimous support from his congressional Republicans that he achieved with ease in the 107th, when the Democrats ran the Senate.

President Bush looked like a colossus astride the American political stage in November 2002. By March 2003, as he struggled to gain support in the United Nations for his Iraq policy, faced open opposition from many House and Senate Republicans to his tax policy, was unable to confirm Miguel Estrada to an appeals court position, lost in the Senate on drilling in the Arctic National Wildlife Refuge, and saw his approval drop to the low or mid-fifties because of public pessimism about the economy, he looked weak and vulnerable. But that rapid shift in the political winds tells us only that predictions about where he, his party, and the opposition Democrats will be in three months, six months, two years, or a decade are folly.

After war with Iraq (just under way as this is written), the president may get a sharp boost in job approval that will translate into momentum and an infusion of political capital, which he will surely use to advance his policy agenda. Some successes there—if accompanied by a robust economic upturn by the spring or early summer of 2004—will leave him and his Republicans well positioned to sweep the board again in the November elections, and in position to transform the policy world in Washington, the international world order, and possibly the alignment of our parties. But the opposite could easily happen. So could a third alternative, perhaps the most likely: continued even divisions between the parties at all levels, close divisions in Congress, and tightly competitive elections for a long time to come.

A Beacon of Hope

Congresswoman Nancy Pelosi

Congresswoman NANCY PELOSI *is the Democratic leader of the U.S. House of Representatives, the highest-ranking woman in the history of the U.S. Congress, and the first woman to lead a major political party.*

She has served in the House for sixteen years, representing California's 8th Congressional District, which includes most of the city of San Francisco. Congresswoman Pelosi's priorities are safety and soundness for the American people—keeping our homeland safe and making our economy sound. As Democratic leader, her goal is to ensure that the American people have a clear understanding of Democratic plans to promote and protect the public and grow the economy.

THROUGHOUT ITS GLORIOUS HISTORY, THE DEMOCRATIC PARTY has been blessed with brilliant leaders who have galvanized our party and led the American people on a path to hope, opportunity, and prosperity. Presidents Franklin D. Roosevelt and John F. Kennedy, Speaker Tip O'Neill, Congresswoman Barbara Jordan, and San Francisco's own, Congressman Phil Burton, are just a few of the names that have made our party the beacon of hope for so many. Through their leadership and the dedication of activists nationwide, we remain the party that reflects the greatness of America and its people.

As we say in my home state of California, the beauty is in the mix. From that beauty flows our moral strength, our boundless creativity, and our versatility. We Democrats are proud that our party looks like America. From across the country, from across the political spectrum, we offer such diversity not only of ethnic background, but of philosophy and geography. We are proud that as Democrats, we recognize the barriers to opportunity and we work together to overcome them.

We celebrate the past and will forever hold sacred the principles and values taught to us by our past leaders. Today, however, we are focused on the future. We seek to answer a simple question that is in the hearts of all Americans: During these troubled and often unsettling times, how can we make this country, indeed this world, a better place for our children?

The Democratic Party will succeed in making a better world for our children by focusing on the safety and soundness of the

American people. The Preamble to the United States Constitution states that, as elected officials, our highest priority is to protect the American people. Since the tragic terrorist attacks of September 11, 2001, this has taken on new meaning. We must protect our precious homeland from the threat of terrorism at home as well as military threats from abroad. And as we protect and defend our people and our country, we must also protect and defend the Constitution of the United States and our cherished civil liberties guaranteed therein.

Protecting the safety of the American people goes hand in hand with promoting the soundness of our economy. It is only with economic opportunity—a good job with good pay—that each of us has the chance to live life to its fullest.

Democrats have presented the American people with an economic plan that will first and foremost provide jobs. Job creation is the engine of our economy. Without good-paying jobs, our economy will continue to falter. Throughout history, the Democratic Party has spearheaded the effort for jobs; we are doing so again today.

Any comprehensive economic plan includes the revamping of our health care system for young and old alike, while protecting the cherished programs of Medicare, Medicaid, and Social Security. Affordable, quality health care should be a basic right for all Americans.

Educating the American people—from preschool through lifelong learning—is the most dynamic investment we can make and will strengthen the economy more than any tax incentive. Educating our children is also key to the soundness of the American family. All parents yearn for their children to succeed. Without quality education, our children cannot succeed. Our public schools need the resources for teachers to instruct and children to learn. We must invest in our children, for they are the messengers to a future we will never know.

Throughout recent history, there has been a bipartisan effort to protect our natural resources and our precious planet for the generations to come. Tragically, since the Bush administration came into office, it has rolled back thirty years of bipartisan environmental protections—from clean air to clean water to pristine forests and national parks. America deserves better. Democrats recognize the need for clean water to drink, clean air to breathe, and safe food to eat.

Some say the 2002 election results have sown seeds of doubt about our party. But I prefer to view them as seeds of renewal. As House Democratic leader, I promise this: never again will the Democratic Party go into an election without a Democratic message saying who we are and what we stand for.

We stand for the principles in which we believe—fairness, opportunity, patriotism, community, equal rights, and a strong America, safe and prosperous at home, and committed abroad to a more secure and just world, free from the fear of terrorism.

As a nation, we have great and grave issues to decide—as fateful as any of those faced in our history. So we must reach across party lines as we stand for principle and serve our country together. We will find common ground wherever we can, and stand our ground wherever we must to be true to the people we represent.

As the only woman to lead a major party in the history of the Congress, I am proud of my party for breaking down another barrier and leading America closer to the ideal of equality that is both our heritage and our hope. When I was first elected to party leadership, I received cards and notes from all over the country. Many were from women and girls inspired that my colleagues had shattered a glass ceiling forever. One young girl wrote to me quoting Eleanor Roosevelt, who said: "The future belongs to those who believe in the beauty of their dreams." Implicit in that quote is a challenge for all of us. This is a challenge that the Democratic Party has met and will continue to meet.

The Democratic Party is about the future. We are committed to building a future where all of our children will be able to believe in the beauty of their dreams, and where all our children will have the opportunity to pursue and fulfill those dreams in a secure and prosperous America, in a safe and peaceful world.

The Dysfunction of
America's Political Parties

Peter G. Peterson

PETER G. PETERSON *is chairman and co-founder of the Black-stone Group. He is chairman of the Federal Reserve Bank of New York, chairman of the Council on Foreign Relations, founding chairman of the Institute for International Economics, founding president of the Concord Coalition, and co-chair of the Confer-ence Board Commission on Public Trust and Private Enterprise. Mr. Peterson was chairman and CEO of Lehman Brothers (1973–1984) and chairman and CEO of Bell and Howell Corpo-ration (1963–1971). In 1971, President Richard Nixon named Mr. Peterson assistant to the president for international economic af-fairs. He was named secretary of commerce in 1972.*

Anyone who tries to participate in public affairs will sooner or later face a character-testing question about the right balance between pragmatism and idealism: How much damage will you allow your party to do in order to gain power and accomplish some greater good? Power without principle must be rejected. But then again, principle without power doesn't help much either.

Notwithstanding such reflections, I believe that the integrity of America's two major political parties has so deteriorated that many Americans who once worked, led, and campaigned for them are rethinking their attachment to parties that are no longer principled nor powerful. These Americans once served as full-fledged "Republicans" and "Democrats." But a growing number now doubt their affiliation. They no longer want to belong to either camp—or at least want to remove the insignia from their old uniforms.

In my own case, I have belonged to the Republican Party all my life. As a Republican, I have served as a cabinet member (once), a presidential commission member (three times), an all-purpose political ombudsman (many times), and a relentless crusader whom some would call a crank (throughout). During most of my service, I have been careful to try not to subscribe to any party dogma that violated my common sense, not to assume that a constituency is sacrosanct just because the party says so, and not to believe that the other party is automatically the enemy. Yet that's just the problem. Increasingly, those who serve my party are subject to all of these pressures. And I know many Democrats who feel just as I do about their own party.

Let me illustrate these sentiments from the standpoint of fiscal policy, the area I know best. Among the bedrock principles that the Republican Party has stood for since its very origins in the 1850s is the principle of fiscal stewardship—the idea that government should invest in posterity and safeguard future generations from unsustainable liabilities. It is a priority that has always attracted me to the party. At various times in our history (especially after wars), Republican leaders have honored this principle by advocating and legislating painful budgetary retrenchment, including both spending cuts and tax hikes.

Over the last quarter century, however, the Grand Old Party has abandoned these original convictions. Without ever renouncing stewardship itself—indeed, while talking incessantly about legacies, endowments, family values, and leaving "no child behind"—the GOP leadership has by degrees come to embrace the very different notion that deficit spending is a sort of fiscal wonder drug. Like taking aspirin, you should do it regularly just to stay healthy and do lots of it whenever you're feeling out of sorts.

With the arrival of Ronald Reagan in the White House, this idea was first introduced as part of an extraordinary "supply-side revolution" in fiscal policy, needed (so the thinking ran) as a one-time fix for an economy gripped by stagflation. To those who worried about more debt, they said, Relax, it won't happen—we'll "grow out of it." Over the course of the 1980s, under the influence of this revolution, what grew most was federal debt, from 26 to 43 percent of GDP. During the next decade, GOP leaders became less conditional in their advocacy. Now they argued that deficit finance was nearly always a good strategy, particularly for the sake of tax cuts—though much of this bold talk could be excused as the bluster of a minority party that neither occupied the White House nor called the shots in Congress. Since 2001, the fiscal strategizing of the GOP has ascended to a new level of fiscal irresponsibility. For the first time ever, a Republican leadership in complete control of our national government is advocating a massive and virtually endless policy of debt creation.

The numbers are simply breathtaking. When President George W. Bush entered office, the ten-year budget balance was officially projected to be a surplus of $5.6 trillion—a vast boon to future generations that GOP leaders "firmly promised" would be committed to their benefit by, for example, prefunding the future cost of Social Security. Those promises were quickly forgotten. A large tax cut and continued spending growth, combined with a recession, the shock of 9/11, and the bursting of the stock-market bubble, pulled that surplus down to a mere $1 trillion by the end of 2002. Unfazed by this turnaround, the Bush administration proposed a second tax-cut package in 2003 in the face of huge new fiscal demands, including a war in Iraq and an urgent "homeland security" agenda. By midyear, prudent forecasters pegged the ten-year fiscal projection at a *deficit* of well over $4 trillion (and that includes $2.5 trillion of Social Security surpluses that we promised to keep "locked up").

So there you have it: in just two years there was a $10 trillion swing in the deficit outlook. Coming into power, the Republican leaders faced a choice between tax cuts and providing genuine funding for the future of Social Security (what a landmark reform this would have been!). They chose tax cuts. After 9/11, they faced a choice between tax cuts and getting serious about the extensive measures needed to protect this nation against further terrorist attacks, investments spelled out in chilling detail in the Hart-Rudman Report and by the Council on Foreign Relations. They chose tax cuts. After war broke out in the Middle East, they faced a choice between tax cuts and galvanizing the nation behind a policy of future-oriented burden sharing. Again and again, they chose tax cuts. At a time when the young men and women in our armed forces were being asked to risk the ultimate sacrifice, they boldly asked the rest of us to "sacrifice" by cutting our own taxes. Keep in mind that such tax cutting shifts even more of our future federal spending burden onto these young soldiers' future income—as if they haven't given enough. Keep in mind as well that these young people, according to official Social Security trustees' numbers, will *already* have to pay the equivalent of 25 to 33 percent of their payroll into Social Security and Medicare before they retire just to keep these programs solvent.

Relative to the size of our economy, the recent $10 trillion deficit swing is the largest in U.S. history other than during years of total war. With total war, of course, you have the excuse that you expect the emergency to be over soon and thus be able to pay back the new debt during subsequent years of peace and prosperity. Yet few believe that the major drivers of today's deficit projections, not even the War on Terror, are similarly short-term. Indeed, the biggest single driver of the projections, the growing cost of senior entitlements, is certain to become much worse just beyond the ten-year horizon when the huge baby boom generation starts retiring in earnest.

Two facts left unmentioned in the deficit numbers cited above will help put the cost of the Boomer retirement into focus.

First, the deficit projections would be much larger if we took away the "trust fund surplus" we are supposed to be dedicating to the future of Social Security and Medicare; and second, the size of this trust fund, even if we were really accumulating it—which we are not—is dwarfed by the $25 trillion in total unfunded liabilities still hanging over both programs. A longer time horizon does not justify near-term deficits. If anything, the longer-term demographics are an argument for sizable near-term surpluses.

One might suppose that a reasoned debate over this deficit-happy policy would at least be admissible within the "discussion tent" of the GOP. Apparently, it is not. I've seen Republicans get blackballed for merely observing, in point of fact, that national investment is limited by national savings; that large deficits typically reduce national savings; or that higher deficits eventually trigger higher interest rates (a proposition denied by the recent chairman of the Council of Economic Advisers, until someone pointed out, awkwardly, that he affirmed it himself in a textbook he wrote before joining the administration). I've seen others get pilloried for picking on the wrong constituency—for suggesting, say, that a tax loophole for a corporation or wealthy retiree is no better, ethically or economically, than a dubious welfare program.

For some "supply side" Republicans, the pursuit of lower taxes has evolved into a religion, indeed a tax-cut theology that simply discards any objective evidence that violates the faith. Even after the explosion of federal debt in the eighties, an explosion that supply-siders had predicted would never happen again, their leading prophets seriously urged that we do it all over again.

So long as taxes are cut, even dissimulation is allowable. A new GOP fad is to propose that tax cuts be officially "sunsetted" in two or five or ten years in order to minimize the projected revenue loss—and then go out and tell supporters that, of course, the sunset is not to be taken seriously and that rescinding such tax cuts is politically unlikely. Among themselves, in other words, the loudly whispered message is that a setting sun always rises. In 2001, that's how GOP congressional leaders sold the income tax rate cuts and the estate-tax phaseout; this year, that's how they are selling child credits, an end to the "marriage penalty," and lower taxes on dividends and capital gains. It's as though I were to grant you a mortgage to buy a home and then deny that you are obligated to make any payments beyond the first thirty-six months.

What's remarkable is how so many elected Republicans go along with the charade. The same GOP senators who overwhelmingly approved (without a single nay vote) the Sarbanes-Oxley Act to crack down on shady corporate accounting of investments worth millions of dollars see little wrong with turning around and making utterly fraudulent pronouncements about tax cuts that will cost billions of dollars or, indeed, even trillions of dollars. And these costs will arrive just as the huge boomer bills are coming due. No catastrophe will divert the tax-cutting theologians from their sacred mission.

For other Republicans, all this tax-cutting talk is a mere tactic. I know several brilliant and partisan Republicans who admit to me, in private, that much of what they say about taxes is of course not really true. But, they say, it's the only way to reduce government spending: chop revenue and trust that the Democrats, like Solomon, will agree to cut spending rather than punish our children by smothering them with debt. This clever apologia would be more believable if their party—in all matters *other than* cutting the aggregate tax burden—were to speak loudly and act decisively in favor of deficit reductions. But of course it doesn't.

If you don't believe me on this point, listen instead to Urban Institute tax expert Eugene Steuerle, respected by both parties for his long track record of dispassionate objectivity. To date, Steuerle writes, the Bush administration has assiduously tried "to avoid budget choices that might take some tax or benefit expenditures away from anyone. Thus it has not pushed to enact any systematic reform that almost inevitably creates losers as well as winners. Every significant enactment so far has involved losing revenues by more spending, or tax cuts. So far, few benefits, however unworthy, have been taken away from interest groups—as reflected in the dearth of base-broadening tax proposals. Preferences sought by many groups—farmers, steel workers, and railroads, among others—have often been expanded." In other words, it's hard to find the small-government argument persuasive when, on the spending front, the GOP leaders do nothing to reform entitlements, allow debt-service costs to rise along with the debt, and urge greater spending on defense—and when these three functions comprise over four-fifths of all federal outlays.

The starve-government-at-the-source strategy is not only hypocritical, it is likely to fail—with great injury to the young— once the other party decides to raise the ante rather than play the sucker and do the right thing. When Democratic presidential contender Dick Gephardt proposed a vast new national health insurance plan in the spring of 2003, he justified its $2.5 trillion cost over ten years by suggesting that we "pay" for it by rescinding most of the administration's tax legislation. If it's okay to deficit finance, he reasoned, let's spend the same amount of money on health care rather than tax cuts. Oddly, it never occurred to these GOP strategists that two can play this game.

Not surprisingly, many Democrats have thrown a spotlight on the GOP's irresponsible obsession with tax cutting in order to improve their party's image with voters, even to the extent of billing themselves as born-again champions of fiscal responsibility. Though I welcome any newcomers to the cause of genuine fiscal stewardship, I doubt that the Democratic Party as a whole is any less dysfunctional than the Republican. It's just dysfunctional in a different way.

Yes, the Republican Party line often boils down to cutting taxes and damning the torpedoes. And yes, by whipping up one-sided popular support for lower taxes, the GOP preempts responsible discussion of tax fairness and forces many Democrats to echo weakly, "Me too." But it's equally true that the Democratic Party line often boils down to boosting outlays and damning the torpedoes. Likewise, Democrats regularly short-circuit any prudent examination of the single biggest spending issue, the future of senior entitlements, by castigating all reformers as heartless Scrooges. Social Security, as officially projected, will be able to pay only 74 percent of its now-scheduled benefits by the year 2045. Should we face that fact or bury our heads in the sand?

I have often and at great length criticized the free-lunch games of many GOP reform plans for Social Security—such as personal accounts that will be "funded" by deficit-financed contributions. But at least they pretend to have reform plans. *Democrats have nothing.* Or, as Bob Kerrey puts it quite nicely, most of his fellow Democrats propose the "do-nothing plan," a blank sheet of paper that essentially says it is okay to cut benefits by 26 percent across the board when the money runs out. Assuming that Democrats would feel genuine compassion for the lower-income retirees, widows, and disabled parents who would be most affected by such a cut, I have suggested to them that maybe we ought to introduce an "affluence test" that reduces benefits for fat cats like me. To my amazement, Democrats angrily respond with irrelevant clichés like "programs for the poor are poor programs" or "Social Security is a social contract that cannot be broken." Apparently, it doesn't matter that the program is already unsustainable. They cling to the mast and are ready to go down with the ship. For most Democratic leaders, federal entitlements are their theology.

To be sure, Republicans can be shameless when they dress up tax cuts in patriotic colors—as though accepting a tax *cut* is somehow equivalent to wartime sacrifice. Yet Democrats do the same with entitlement expansions. When they talk fulsomely about their more expensive entitlement proposal, such as a Medicare prescription drug benefit offered as a pure "add on," they like to say it reflects their stronger commitment to the greatness and generosity of America. Either way, it's astonishing that we can congratulate ourselves for civic virtue by giving ourselves bigger presents and sending bigger bills to our kids.

The same goes for national security and sacred-cow interests. Yes, the GOP has its ties to Main Street and Wall Street. But Democrats cling to their own graven images. In the wake of 9/11, for instance, they noisily delayed terrorism insurance until it passed muster with the trial lawyers lobby, and then airport security until it passed muster with the government union lobby. This crass favoritism hurt them in the subsequent 2002 elections. The Republicans, framing the issue as a choice between national security and special interests, were delighted to put them in that box. They knew the Democrats' hands were tied. Core constituencies must be serviced.

What exactly gave rise to this bipartisan flight from integrity and responsibility—and when? That's a large question to ask about a profound institutional trend that's been with us for at least a quarter of a century. My own theory, for what it's worth, is that it got started during the "Me Decade" of the 1970s, when a socially fragmenting America began to gravitate around a myriad of interest groups, each more fixated on pursuing and financing, through massive political campaign contributions, its own agenda than in safeguarding the common good of the nation. Political parties, rather than helping to transcend these fissures and bind the country together, instead began to cater to them and ultimately sold themselves out. The new business of electioneering, redistricting, raising money, trading favors, and servicing contributors began to eclipse the old business of doing what's right for the country.

Along the way, as the parties lost their conscience and their legitimacy, so too did they lose their unifying principles and their political power, their ability to galvanize the nation to move in a better direction. Regrettably, to the extent they now exercise power, they often end up doing serious injury to the very constituencies they pledge to help. The Republicans champion a family-oriented opportunity society, yet busily rig the economy with debt explosives that sabotage every parent's hopes to raise capital for a new business or pass on assets to their children. The

Democrats champion the working and middle classes, yet happily steer their New Deal entitlement ship of state, with all of its top-heavy new rigging, toward an unyielding demographic iceberg that threatens to leave these hardworking Americans adrift without a lifeboat.

I'm not sure what it will take to make our two-party system healthy again. Hopefully, we will see party heads on both sides make truces with each other for the purpose of binding up the wounds of dysfunctional partisanship. Among the many possible motivations for such truces, perhaps the most reliable is enlightened self-interest. In the search for a durable majority, Republicans will sooner or later realize that it won't happen without coming to terms with deficits and debts, and Democrats will likewise realize it won't happen for them without coming to terms with entitlements.

The emergence of a new and rousing battle to win the affections of the middle of the electorate would be good for both parties. So would a healthier competition for social "influencers." As more of our nation's civic, philanthropic, and commercial leadership drifts away from national party politics, party heads will sooner or later understand the cost of taking their elite cadre for granted. I'm pleased to have been involved in catalyzing one such effort, the Concord Coalition, a national bipartisan organization dedicated to fiscal sanity. To me, it shows what can happen when our most talented and accomplished citizens—and I'm talking about the likes of former senators Warren Rudman, Paul Tsongas, Sam Nunn, Bob Kerrey, as well as Paul Volcker, Bob Rubin, and Lloyd Cutler—choose to withdraw from government service and seek other constructive venues for public discussion. They feel liberated, they ask the right questions, they kindle honest debate, and they start attracting sympathetic listeners. Invariably, they begin to force party heads to reach out in their direction.

Whether any of this happens sooner or later, of course, ultimately depends upon the voters. In a special-interest society, it's the electorate that must help make politics safe for the general-interest candidate. And as eras change, so too do generations of electorates. Our parties began to grow dysfunctional in a bygone era of social and cultural upheaval that was accompanied by the emergence of cynicism and disengagement among young voters. Amid the very different mood of post–9/11 America, perhaps we will soon witness the emergence of a new and very different crop of young voters—who are freshly engaged in mainstream politics and will start holding candidates to a more rigorous and objective standard of integrity. That would be good news indeed for the future of our parties. In any case, I fervently hope that America does not have to drift into real trouble, either at home or abroad, before our leaders get "scared straight" and stop playing chicken with one another. That's a risky course, full of possible disasters. It's not a solution that a great nation like ours ought to be counting on.

America Is Hurting

Dennis Rivera

Currently serving as president of 1199 SEIU, New York's Health and Human Service Union, where he represents more than 240,000 health care workers from throughout the state of New York, DENNIS RIVERA also serves as chair of the health care division for the Service Employees International Union, which represents 1.8 million workers nationwide. A former member of the Democratic National Committee, Rivera is credited with developing 1199 SEIU into what the press and political insiders cite as New York's most politically powerful union.

WHILE WARS AGAINST TERRORISM AND IRAQ HAVE HOGGED THE headlines for the past couple of years, most Americans have been the victims of a different war. The Bush administration has gone to battle against the standard of living of the vast majority of Americans, and it has trained its fire on the very assumptions on which that standard of living is based.

Unless the Democratic Party recognizes this and takes its place more forcefully on the economic battlefield, it is doomed again and again to shameful losses like those of November 2002.

The Democratic Party is on the verge of irrelevance. Suffering millions look to it for leadership . . . and too often get silence. With a few honorable exceptions, the party of the New Deal and the Fair Deal today seems capable of nothing more than the political deal.

Look around at the shambles of our nation's economy.

States and local communities struggle with deficits that in 2004 will total $80 billion. Headlines tell of closed hospitals and firehouses, shorter school years, laid-off teachers and social workers, slashed police and environmental services, and gutted programs for children, seniors, and the poor. Some states are even emptying their prisons.

Unemployment keeps rising. The stock market keeps falling. The national debt is at an all-time peak.

The richest 1 percent of the population controls about 40 percent of the nation's wealth. Nothing better illustrates the arrogance at the top than the secret deal made recently by American Airlines executives. While unionized workers reluctantly approved deep contract givebacks, American's top brass were giving themselves huge bonuses (later canceled after an outcry by the union) and guaranteed pensions.

The inequities in our health care system are a national disgrace. One of every six Americans (and one of nine health care workers) has no medical insurance. As a nation we spend 14 percent of our gross domestic product on health care, far more than any other country. But the ordinary American is paying more for less. Job-linked health coverage is shrinking as co-pays skyrocket. Prescriptions are too often out of reach for our parents. And while we led the world in life expectancy fifty years ago, in 1997 American women ranked twentieth among industrialized nations and American men ranked twenty-second.

President Bush's budget for fiscal year 2004 proposed to eliminate health coverage for 13.6 million children, reduce food stamp benefits, and end school lunches for 2.4 million low-income children. Increasingly, our children begin their lives in poverty and our seniors end their lives in despair.

How did we get into this mess?

The seeds for our current problems were sown back in the Reagan years with attacks on unions, big military-fueled budget deficits, tax breaks for the rich, deregulation, and slashed social programs. But George W. Bush has taken things a giant step farther. He and his radical right ideologues want to repeal the entire twentieth century.

The last century produced a loose social contract based on government's role in advancing the American Dream of widely shared prosperity. Among the pillars of that social contract were progressive taxation, a social safety net to protect the most vulnerable Americans, the right of workers to organize into unions, and a whole network of programs to protect the environment, public health, and consumers, and to secure the rights of minorities, women, immigrants, and other groups that have experienced discrimination.

If the Bush administration has its way, this entire fabric of government-propelled programs will be shredded and discarded. This process is already well under way, advanced by the twin engines of militarism and tax cuts.

The president's messianic approach to international relations is moving us toward a permanent state of war. The main things wrong with this, of course, are killing innocent people and possibly incinerating the planet. But our move toward militarism is also enriching the president's friends while leaving little left over for social programs.

And what little is left over is made even smaller by the president's radical tax program. Bush wants to end the dividend tax and estate tax. He wants to give personal income tax breaks that would save the wealthiest 1 percent of Americans an average of $80,000 a year. These changes would come on top of a reduction in corporate tax rates from 50 percent of total taxes paid in 1940 to about 14 percent today. The net effect of all of this would be to erase a concept that goes back at least as far as 1913, when the income tax was established. That concept held that in common we share a society that enables some to amass more wealth than others, and that those whom society smiles upon economically should give back accordingly.

The Bush ideologues hate this idea. Their fury over taxes and big government translates into a reverse Robin Hood program that steals from the poor and gives to the rich. But tragically, many who are stolen from continue to vote for additional larceny. There's a deep strain of American individualism that is suspicious of government and hostile to taxes. The radical Republicans know very well how to tap into these emotions. Our job is to create a different model that appeals to a more realistic, humane, and life-affirming set of emotions.

Polls show that the majority of Americans disapprove of Bush's domestic policies. People who are working two jobs and still falling behind, people who have been out of work for months and years, people who have lost their pensions and can't afford health care—people like these understand that something is wrong. They're ready to do something about it. But most of them haven't been shown a practical alternative.

What do they do? They drop out. They grow cynical about politics and stay home on Election Day. They are convinced that big money controls our electoral process, and who can tell them they're wrong? They believe that pulling the lever for Tweedledum or Tweedledee is an exercise in futility.

But what would happen if a new Democratic Party emerged out of the ashes of the old, championing those who have been left out? What would happen if that invigorated party told the story of unions that have lifted people out of poverty, helped assimilate immigrants, and provided health care coverage and secure retirements? What if that party said unequivocally that justice has not been fully done for minorities, women, and others who have suffered discrimination, and that we must not stop until full justice is won? What if that party proudly reviewed the record of the Wagner Act, the Social Security Act, the Civil Rights Act, the Environmental Protection Agency, and the hundreds of other legislative and regulatory initiatives through which Americans have improved their lives through the agency of government? What if that party vowed not to shrink from its own best traditions of concern for the needy, but to return to them with bold and renewed vigor?

If the Democratic Party moved in this direction, it would activate the disaffected millions who today sit on the sidelines or vote Republican. It would call home its core membership and create a new and invincible constituency. Of course, there's another alternative. The Democrats could continue as they are now and disappear into the historical cubbyhole occupied by the Whigs, Federalists, and Greenbacks.

We're poised at a crossroads. There's a lot at stake. I'm betting that President Bush's economic war against Americans will produce a domestic groundswell ready to build a better America. Let's hope the Democratic Party is ready to help harness that energy and get the job done.

Democratic Politics
in the Age of Terror

Congressman Joe Scarborough

Former congressman JOE SCARBOROUGH *(R-FL) hosts* Scarborough Country, *providing on-air commentary and analysis, and his nightly* Real Deal.

Scarborough's experience has included guest-hosting spots on all the major cable news networks and many other guest appearances on both network and cable news programs. Most recently, he was a guest host on Nachman *as well as other live news specials for MSNBC.*

Joe Scarborough served as a member of Congress from 1994 to 2001. After leaving office, he was named by President Bush as a member of the president's Council on the 21st Century Work-

force, where he serves with Labor Secretary Chao, national labor officials, and business leaders. While in the United States House of Representatives, Joe Scarborough served on the Judiciary Committee and the Armed Services Committee.

Currently, Scarborough is also a partner with Levin, Papantonio, where he concentrates his practice in environmental law.

WHILE IN NEW YORK RECENTLY, MY WIFE AND I DECIDED TO TAKE a walk through Central Park. But as we approached its southwest corner, an unmarked bus stopped beside us and began spitting out military troops. A minute later, fifty or so soldiers with automatic weapons in hand began taking up positions across the great park.

So much for unwinding with a casual Saturday evening stroll.

A female tourist walking next to us watched the troops stream across the area and then grabbed my arm.

"What the hell was that?"

"No idea."

Since New Yorkers seemed to take the Central Park invasion in stride, we continued our trek to the Upper West Side. But watching a springtime stroll morph into a military maneuver brought home just how much American life has changed in the past few years. Those changes have transformed the way we all live, the way we think, and yes, the way we vote.

It shouldn't surprise anyone that the cataclysmic events of September 11 impacted American politics—just as World War II and the Great Depression did during the last century. But even I have been surprised by the Democrats' flat-footed response to the dawning of America's Age of Terror.

Despite their historic rout in the 2002 midterm elections, Democrats need not despair. Instead, they need to look no further than Bill Clinton's 1992 victory to find, in the words of Bruce Springsteen, a reason to believe.

The story is well known. A president, made seemingly invincible by a victorious war, soon became politically obsolete.

George Bush never saw Bill Clinton coming, any more than Winston Churchill imagined being deposed by the likes of Clement Attlee months after the British prime minister saved the world from Adolf Hitler's thousand-year reich.

But make no mistake. Bush and Churchill fell from grace not because of sagging markets or high unemployment, but because the wars they helped win ushered in a new age neither understood.

By now we've all heard that it was "the economy, stupid" that elected Bill Clinton. And perhaps the flat American economy did put the Arkansas governor over the top of the polls. But it was another historical event that made Clinton's ascent to the White House even remotely possible.

David Halberstam's *War in a Time of Peace* explains that Bush was unprepared for the brave new world that accompanied the Soviet Union's collapse on Christmas Day 1991. I suspect that Bush 41 still wonders at times how the American people could have rejected a World War II fighter pilot—and a conquering hero of the Evil Empire—for the likes of Bill Clinton.

But there are no victory laps in American politics. America's forty-year struggle against the Soviet Union ended and the good guys won. Americans quickly turned their gaze elsewhere.

Without an Evil Empire, there was no longer the need for a conquering hero. With the world no longer a pushed button away from nuclear extinction, Americans didn't seem to mind that blue jeans, pizza, and frat-house pastimes replaced the almost puritanical structure of George Bush's White House. To paraphrase Peggy Noonan, the Soviets' collapse meant that character was no longer king.

But today's Democratic Party leaders must recognize that September 11 restored that lost quality to its throne.

The Party of Clinton can seize power back from Bush 43 and the gangs of Republicans now dominating the federal government. But to do so, they must find their focus, change their tactics, and embrace the realities facing Americans in this new Age of Terror.

Democratic strategists must also steal the political playbook of a politician they hate—former speaker Newt Gingrich.

Gingrich's Republican class of 1993 had much in common with Tom Daschle and Nancy Pelosi's Democratic class of 2003. Like Republicans a decade ago, Daschle Democrats are irrelevant, devoid of power, and consigned to doing little more than causing the occasional delay of a judicial nominee.

But unlike the Gingrich gang of 1993, Democrats today have no message, no vision, and no road map to guide them from the political wilderness where they find themselves stranded.

So for the sake of a fair fight in 2004 and beyond, below is a Republican's road map for the Democrats' return to power:

1. Stand for Something, Stupid

It's a radical notion, I know. But telling Americans what your party believes is something the Democratic Party has somehow overlooked lately. Maybe the message is muddled because they don't *know* what they believe. Or perhaps they do, but don't want Americans finding out what it is.

Regardless, Democrats would be wise to follow Gingrich's Contract with America model to focus their efforts and have their message reach America.

The Democratic Party's values must be put to paper clearly and concisely, and their creed should fit neatly on a bumper sticker. Ten years ago, Gingrich Republicans preached "less taxes, less spending, less regulations." One year later, they regained Congress for the first time in forty years.

At present, there is no slogan, no sentence, no treatise to summarize the Daschle Democrats' agenda in the Age of Terror. That is, of course, grim news for Democratic candidates up for election in 2004.

The Republican Party's greatest fear is that one day soon, Democrats in Washington will turn their gaze away from their Lava lamps long enough to notice that the world—and America—has changed radically since Woodstock. Today, Americans are a helluva lot more concerned about national security, homeland security, and economic security than abortion rights, gay rights, or illegal immigrants' civil rights.

Whether Tom Daschle, Nancy Pelosi, or John Kerry like it or not, that is the political reality Democrats face heading into 2004. Arguing about gay-adoption rights or partial birth abortion is so 1998.

Democrats need to get over it. The twentieth century is history.

2. Get Over It, the 1960s Are Over

Time magazine's Joe Klein nailed it. The Democratic Party seems to be led by aging hippies who detest all things martial. This unfortunate political instinct springs from the Vietnam era, when a generation of college students railed against what they considered to be an unjust war. That antiwar movement took on all the urgency of a moral crusade (except, of course, for all the sex, drugs, and rock and roll that accompanied the protests).

Who knows why, but in between their efforts to take over college campuses and levitate the Pentagon, those activists protesting against Vietnam still haven't grasped three political truths from that era:

1. Most Americans still blame those protests for America's defeat in Vietnam and the deaths of young American soldiers.
2. Even when 60 percent opposed America's actions in Vietnam, half of those polled thought our government should have been more aggressive in its execution of the war.
3. If you still can't bring yourself to face the realities of truths 1 and 2, consider this. At the height of the peace movement, prowar candidate Richard Nixon obliterated the Democrats' dove, George McGovern, in one of the United States' greatest political landslides ever.

Republican strategists figured this stuff out thirty years ago! That's why Republican candidates have been feasting off of Democratic "wimps" for thirty years now. Meanwhile, survivors of the peace movement leading the Democratic Party continue embracing their romanticized view of the sixties instead of facing up to the cold realities of twenty-first-century politics.

Sorry to bring the bad news, but college students today trust the military more than their liberal history professors.

Hey, I'm sure the sex was great, the pot was pure, and the music was *killer*. But, dude, move on. The sixties are over.

3. The Power of Positive Thinking

They won't admit it publicly, but get them alone when their defenses are down, and most Democratic strategists will admit that their party needs a sagging economy or another terrorist attack on America to regain control of Congress and the White House.

Democrats need not be offended and Republicans need not pretend to be shocked. After all, it was Jimmy Carter's policy failures that elected Ronald Reagan. And who could forget Newt Gingrich blaming the murder of two young boys by their mother on failed Democratic policies.

But crass opportunism is never a viable alternative to a coherent political strategy. Yet the Democrats face further irrelevance if the economy rebounds and terror attacks are forestalled. This is no way to run a national party.

Democrats must shake their thirty-year rap as naysayers who "blame America first" to transform themselves in this area, forget following the Gingrich example, and turn instead to Ronald Reagan. Bill Clinton did, and look at what it got him.

By telling Americans that they will strengthen the country's national and economic security based on their policies instead of George Bush's miscues, Democratic candidates can deliver their message to a receptive America. And assume then that, in the words of Ronald Reagan, America's greatest days truly do lie ahead.

And in the Age of Terror, that's a message that will find receptive ears.

Slap the Donkey Till It Kicks

Reverend Al Sharpton

Reverend AL SHARPTON is the president of the National Action Network, an author, and presidential candidate for the 2004 Democratic nomination.

WHEN I CAME OF AGE TO VOTE, I REMEMBER ASKING MY MOTHER, "Why are we Democrats?" She responded, "Because it is the party for regular people like us." I had this discussion with her in our small apartment in the Brownsville section of Brooklyn, New York, where I was born and reared. However, my mother was born and reared in Dothan, Alabama, under strict laws of racial segregation. Among other things, this meant that she could not vote until well beyond her achieving the legal age at that time. This meant the right to vote, and the subsequent choice of the party she enrolled in, was very important to her. In her day it was clear that the Democratic Party stood for pro-labor, pro–civil rights, pro–women's rights, pro–minimum wage, and pro–social justice issues. Today, we are not so clear on what we stand for. We, in the pursuit of new "swing" voters, we have abandoned *core* principles and, therefore, lost a clear and energized *core* constituency. We have no value if we imitate the Republicans. People always prefer authentic people over imitators. But we lose something more important. We lose our soul. To operate effectively in the twenty-first century, we must save the soul of the party that we believe in, the principles that make us Democrats in the first place. There is nothing more ridiculous than this parade of elephants walking around in donkey jackets.

In the mid-eighties, there was a deliberate effort by some moderate forces to move the party to the right (they would say center). The argument raised was that the party must win the South and the white male vote. In order to do this, they began to support right-wing positions like a military buildup, NAFTA, GATT, the death penalty, equivocation on affirmation action, and some right to organize working laws. Though we won the White House (in no small part due to the presence of Ross Perot in the race), we could not maintain a congressional majority or a Senate majority. Our strategy was flawed. The reason it was not workable is that its assumption was that while we moved away from labor minorities, working-class families, gays and lesbians, and civil libertarians, these groups would be blindly loyal and await our return. As we courted swing voters, who failed to be swayed, we had an erosion of our *core* constituency.

As we approach 2004 and beyond, the political landscape is clear. War is blazing in Iraq. The economy is troubled in the United States: record state budget deficits topped by a historic federal budget deficit, mammoth tax cuts for the wealthy, deregulation of business, the consolidation of media ownership, the nomination of right-wing judges to the federal bench, the attempts to repeal laws that regulate big business's abuse of the environment, the court test on affirmative action, and the creeping congressional campaign to limit women's right to choose, in the name of opposing "partial birth abortion." It is clear that the lines are drawn on what the political issues are but, more important, what's the political philosophy of the day will rule the day. The Democratic Party has a tremendous opportunity to recapture its soul, define its purpose, and bring home in massive numbers the *real* Democrats that have been disappointed. These people did not defect; they felt the party abandoned them.

I call on the party to clearly stand for the following principles. We must not be tentative or vague in our stand. We must be clear and unequivocal.

We should oppose unprovoked military action. The Bush war in Iraq was wrong and unnecessary. It is becoming the Vietnam of the twenty-first century. We should be unequivocal in challenging the Republicans' inconsistent foreign policy, e.g., North Korean policy as opposed to Iraqi policy. We must also challenge the blatant hypocrisy of a party that preaches "balanced budget" sermons while they cause the greatest deficit spending in history. How come we are not pressing them on how, with record state budget deficits, Bush can ask for $75 billion for the first thirty days of war and at the same time propose a $14 billion cut on veterans' programs in his budget plan to Congress?

We must strongly oppose this tax-cut trickle-down economic theory. It does not revive the economy. It does not help middle-class or needy Americans. It only helps the wealthiest Americans, and ultimately they are not helped by a dwindling middle class that produces a weak consumer base for their businesses. We should strongly advocate job creation programs. I have strongly supported Felix Rohatyn's plan of infrastructure redevelopment as I toured the nation. A five-year, $250 billion plan at $50 billion a year added to the federal deficit to rebuild the highways, roadways, tunnels, bridges, and—with an eye on *homeland security*—the ports. The jobs created would expand our tax base, which would more than repay the $250 billion investment.

We must fight for the regulation of big business. Deregulation helped lead to Enron, WorldCom, and other corporate debacles. We must also strongly fight for federal laws with strong federal enforcement of workers' rights to organize. I also feel we must raise the minimum wage by $2.00.

As we help lead the nation in the war against terrorism, we must also oppose any erosion of civil liberties or civil rights. We cannot preach to the world that we must protect "the land of the free and the home of the brave" yet suspend freedom and dare Americans not to be brave enough to question it. The Patriot Act and Anti-Terrorist Act have some stunning parts including allowing detention without charging a person with a crime and the right of government to eavesdrop on lawyer/client conversations. We must protect American rights as the reason for our allies to join us in the fight against terrorism.

Lastly, we must strongly support affirmative action. We cannot equivocate about the need to finish the drive toward full equality and fairness in this nation. We are the party that helped this nation move forward on the issues of racism, sexism, and homophobia. We cannot, in the name of appealing to conservatism, abandon that now. What makes us real Democrats is what we stand for, not trying to placate bigots in hopes of gaining cheap votes.

Dr. Martin Luther King, Jr., used to describe two types of leaders. Thermometers measure the temperature and move based on the climate of the day. But then there are thermostat leaders that change the temperature, that change the political climate to make progress more possible. For the good of the party, the nation, and the world, we must stop reading the temperature and start changing the temperature, to secure a better, more secure world for us all.

Ending Poverty and Ignorance: Transforming American Society from the Perspective of the Hip-Hop Generation

Russell Simmons

RUSSELL SIMMONS *is a master visionary who has shaped the cutting edge of hip-hop—the preeminent force in American popular culture—for the past two decades, during which he founded Def Jam Records, the most successful hip-hop label in history, as well as the Phat Farm clothing line, which sets the hottest trends on the street today. While maintaining his unquestioned status as "the godfather of hip-hop," in recent years, Russell Simmons has transformed himself into the ultimate political activist and philanthropist. He has worked tirelessly to energize and motivate young people—the hip-hop generation—to stand up, mobilize, and "move as an army" to make their voices heard and their votes count.*

WHILE AMERICAN SOCIETY STANDS IN THE FIRST DECADE OF THE twenty-first century as the most technologically advanced and militarily superior society in the world, the national leadership has not been willing to focus public policy, or to commit adequate resources, to winning the war on poverty and ignorance inside the United States. Millions of youths who identify with hip-hop culture, not only in America but also throughout the world, see the inextricable link between American domestic and foreign policies.

A nation that does not put a priority on ending poverty and ignorance amid its own people at home will invariably export that same attitude of neglect to the plight of the poor and impoverished abroad.

Two years ago, we established the Hip-hop Summit Action Network to increase national public awareness on the issues that the hip-hop community affirms as the priority. There are a multitude of different national and international issues that warrant the concern and attention of all people of goodwill. Yet we believe that among those issues, there is none more important than ending poverty and ignorance.

The latest report on poverty issued by the U.S. Census Bureau revealed that after overall poverty in America had slightly declined for four straight years, the nation's poverty rate began to increase from 11.3 percent in 2000 to 11.7 percent in 2001, which represented an increase of 1.3 million persons in poverty in just that one year. In 2003, the poverty rate is now well over 12 percent of the entire U.S. population, which amounts to more than 35 million Americans. Thus, we have begun this century with an unprecedented rate of increase in domestic poverty.

Some have asked why the poetry, lyrics, and music of contemporary hip-hop often portray the harsh, cold realities of urban life. There needs to be a better understanding and appreciation of the fact that our poetry and music reflect and challenge the contradictions of society while at the same time expressing higher aspirations for social, economic, and political change.

Remember that more than one-third of all those who are entrapped in poverty today in the United States are children. Add to that the grossly inadequate funding for public schools in every major metropolitan area across the nation and the growing direct correlation between multitudes of youths being denied an equal high-quality education and the rapid rise in juvenile incarceration in every state. For too many the American Dream has become the American nightmare.

The responsible action for both Democrats and Republicans, as well as for independents, is to view the perplexities of American poverty and social dislocation as a mandate for social transformation. In other words, the old political rhetoric of the past century will not receive an enthusiastic response from today's youth. Hip-hop is about telling and listening to the truth. It is about rising above the restrictions and repressions of the old world order. The American Dream can be and should be redeemed.

We will not be able to make Iraq or any other place in the world an example of participatory democracy where freedom, justice, and equality reign until we are committed to practice at home what we preach aboard. Allowing the current povertization of our society to go unchallenged is an affront to human decency and the single most serious detriment to progress.

There are millions of youths who would like to become involved in improving the conditions of their families and communities in every town, city, and state. We cannot afford inaction due to a perceived generation gap or a cultural gap between youth and elders. What gaps do exist should and can be bridged through encouraging and engaging young grassroots activists, community leaders, artists, and other cultural workers in programs, projects, and actions that empower youth to speak out and take an active ongoing leadership role in the life of their communities.

We visit numerous local schools and communities and we take the time to listen to youths, who have great ideas and energy to help find more effective solutions to the problems of inadequate schools, jobs, housing, health care, and safe environments. Too often when the attributes of poverty are discussed, there is a tendency to blame the victims for their victimization. Too often there is the tendency to blame youths or their culture and way of life for the social conditions that they are consigned to.

Hip-hop continues to grow as a cultural phenomenon globally. As youth around the world seek to relate to hip-hop culture in America, we intend to help transform America into a better place where freedom, justice, and equality are not just out-of-reach ideals but the fundamental reality experienced by all without limitation of race, gender, creed, or color.

We intend to mobilize millions of youths to register to vote utilizing hip-hop as the motivating force before the 2004 elections. The Recording Industry Association of America (RIAA) has already documented that hip-hop artists financially give back to their communities more than artists in any other genre of music. This does not mean, though, that we intend to let the municipal, state, and federal governments off the hook of responsibility. Poverty and ignorance are problems requiring governmental commitment and action together with the responsive actions of individuals and organizations.

The political debate of 2004 will hear the clarion voice of youth who desire to make a difference. We will not permit our views to be ignored or silenced by the political establishment. Our political action committees, grassroots organizing street teams, and cadres of activists will be joined by politically conscious poets and artists and others as we build a new national movement for social transformation.

There is no room for pessimism or a noncaring hopelessness in our consciousness as the immediate future is envisioned. The opportunities to change America in 2004 and beyond far outweigh the forces of intransigence and indifference. The political setbacks of the past can and will be overcome by the empowerment of millions of new young voters who have an irrepressible passion for peace, freedom, and equal justice. The hip-hop generation will rise to this occasion.

Let us stand together. Let us pray together. Let us organize and mobilize together. Let us all work hard together until the victory over poverty and ignorance is finally won.

Why Young Americans
Hate Politics

Ganesh Sitaraman and Previn Warren

*GANESH SITARAMAN is studying government and international re-
lations at Harvard University and is the former chairman of the
Harvard Political Union. PREVIN WARREN is studying modern in-
tellectual history and social thought at Harvard University, and is
the codirector of the Harvard Progressive Advocacy Group. They
are the editors of* Invisible Citizens: Youth Politics After September 11 *(iUniverse, 2003).*

THE NOVEMBER 2002 MIDTERM ELECTIONS HAVE BEEN OF INTER-
est to most commentators primarily because of the heavy losses
faced by the Democratic Party. But a crucial aspect of the elec-

tions has been looked on with little more than silence—the alarming absence of youth voters. Only 32 percent of young Americans aged eighteen to twenty-four were registered to vote in the elections, and only 17 percent voted—compared to 39 percent of Americans of all ages. Now, for most political scientists, the absence of youth participation in this particular election doesn't seem like much of a surprise. It is common wisdom that young people are apathetic and politically lazy, and that they are too hypnotized by MTV culture to care about voting. But if we approach this statistic with any kind of context in mind, there does seem to be something surprising going on. After all, given the patriotism induced by September 11 and the War on Terrorism, one might have expected the long-awaited influx of young people into the civic arena. But alas, things didn't play out the way they should have, and by November 2002 young people were right back where they've been for the past decade—ignored, marginalized, and politically uninterested. So, while pundits pore over the Democrats' fate at the polls, it is distressing that so few have bothered to raise the arguably more pressing question: Why don't young people vote?[1]

Although young people do exhibit low voter turnout rates, the often-proffered explanation that they are "just apathetic" does not hold water. Young people are actually some of the most active members of their communities and are devoting increasing amounts of their time to community service and volunteering. In 2002, 61 percent of college students volunteered in direct service

---

[1] Portions of this essay are adapted from *Invisible Citizens: Youth Politics After September 11,* eds. Ganesh Sitaraman and Previn Warren. New York: iUniverse, 2003. Essay copyright: President and Fellows of Harvard College, 2003.

work, and within that group nearly 90 percent volunteered in high school as well. Moreover, 84 percent believe community volunteerism is an effective way of solving important national issues. But if young people are so pro-active, why don't they vote? And more important, why aren't they engaged in the political process at a more general level?

The cause of youth disengagement from politics stems from what young people perceive to be an irresolvable dichotomy between service and government. Engaging in hands-on community-building projects at soup kitchens or shelters, for example, leads to tangible, immediate results. Participants are able to make a direct impact on the lives of the disadvantaged and can deal directly with issues they care about. The results of service work seem to be unequivocally positive, and volunteers are able to conceptualize the change they've made in society because the beneficiaries always have names and faces. Government work, on the other hand, offers none of these benefits. The public face of politics is the election—characterized by negative advertising, a preponderance of corporate campaign money, and poll-driven leadership. Politics presents itself to young people in ways that confirm their skepticism about government work, which seems to subordinate the common good to special interests and reelection concerns. This is a view of politics that surely is generated in part from political realities. Unfortunately, the consequence of this perception has not been a call to arms among young people to change or revise the system, but rather a renunciation of politics altogether—both its unsavory bureaucratic elements and its ability to act as a crucial, lasting force for social change. Young people have interpreted offensive political abnormalities as "business as usual," rather than seeing them as wholly changeable political aberrations that can and should be challenged. The corollary of this is that they have also largely ignored attempts among politicians to revise the system, seeing the very acts of legislating and lobbying as already bound within a corrupt framework.

While our generation's initiative and resolve in community service work is to be lauded, our inability to shed our fundamentally skewed image of government is both lamentable and dangerous. It is lamentable because it bars us from our country's most effective and fundamental tool for change and perpetuates a cycle of negligence between youth and America's leaders. It is dangerous because it sustains our perceived gap between government and service, a gap that may compromise the long-term vitality of our democratic state. Sadly, young people do not seem to be getting closer to making the connection that government can and should be a force for positive social and political change in America. Like many citizens, they feel an increasing gulf separating them from the decisions being made by their leaders. Moreover, young people in particular have been routinely denied ready access to legitimate information about politics, through the steady trivialization of television news content and the atrophying of public school civics curricula. Perhaps as important, they have experienced less and less "face time" with their government. Sixty-two percent of people under thirty say they were never asked to consider working in government while they were in high school or college.[2] Seventy-eight percent claim that their fellow

---

[2] "Young Americans' Call to Public Service," Hart-Teeter Study for the Council for Excellence in Government, May 2002.

---

students are not well informed about programs such as Ameri-Corps, VISTA, and the Peace Corps, arguably some of the most effective means of directly bringing young people into the realm of public service.[3] In short, young people are not approaching politics because politics is failing to approach them.

Engaging and inspiring young people into civic engagement are not impossible goals, but they will require commitment and devotion to specific initiatives and actions. Policy makers and politicians can immediately take three specific steps to increase youth engagement in the political process.

First, politicians need to spend more time in contact with young people. Over 90 percent of youth believe that increased contact with elected and appointed officials would increase their collective participation in politics. But in addition to addressing young people in schools, communities, and colleges, politicians must inform youth of the opportunities that government service provides. If asked, nearly one-quarter of students would participate in political campaigns—a significant figure given that only 9 percent were actually involved in 2002. Paying attention to young people and asking them to take an active role in government will profoundly increase youth engagement.

Second, our current educational system needs to place a greater emphasis on building citizens. Public schools must teach comprehensive civics courses that not only include the fundamentals of American political institutions and how they create practical social and political change but also outline the basic ways

3 "Volunteerism, Education, and the Shadow of September Eleventh," Leon and Sylvia Panetta Institute for Public Policy, May 2002.

students can become involved. Colleges and universities should take this a step further and offer academic credit for students who participate in political work.

Third, government must address the fiscal barrier to entry into the political sphere. With salary levels in business, law, and medicine multiple times higher than levels in public sector work, many students naturally prefer the Firm to the Capitol, and Wall Street to K Street. In addition to increasing salary levels across the board, government should offer more reciprocal agreement opportunities like the State Department's, by which departments and agencies pay for college education in return for a commitment to work for that agency for three to five years. Furthermore, the military should provide an opportunity within its reciprocal agreement program for students who do not wish to serve in combat directly, but are interested in communications and policy. Not only would this increase youth engagement, but it would also help counter the crisis government faces over the next ten years as baby boomers retire.

While these specific programs will create a noticeable and substantial increase in youth civic involvement, they are not enough in and of themselves to eradicate the kind of civic malaise that adults identify within our generation. Without broader and more substantial reforms in American political culture, it is unlikely that young people will transform themselves into a body of responsible, informed, and compassionate citizens and leaders. Politicians must strike the difficult balance of acting pro-actively on their own initiative and listening to the body of citizens they are supposed to represent. But this balance itself seems to be in question when leaders stop listening to citizens for an articulation and assessment of society's needs and wants. Corporate culture has invaded politics, and the result has been a top-down strategy that seeks to persuade rather than lead and that treats citizens primarily as consumers. Under this approach, people are no longer listened to so they can be represented, but rather so they can be more effectively marketed to. Under this style of politics, proactive leadership is replaced by persuasion, the end goal of which is the self-perpetuation of those in power.

It is clear what must happen, but it is unclear whether anyone will have the courage to do it. Major reforms have to be made in the areas of campaign finance and election advertising. Media executives must have the courage to make a decisive shift in programming, to present accurate and fair coverage of substantive news rather than the type of spectacle that best sells advertisements. Politicians themselves must rethink the culture in which they operate and place a new emphasis on integrity, vision, compassion, and courage rather than polls, insider politics, and spin.

Young people spend their lives inundated by advertising, which has bred in them a genuine mistrust toward gimmicks and the easy sell. They know that something is wrong when the choice between pop music divas and between political candidates looks, feels, and operates in an almost identical fashion. But if their experiences working in communities have told them any one thing, it is that politics is *not* an idle form of consumerism. In choosing overwhelmingly to visit shelters and kitchens instead of the polls, young people are in fact voting—for real people and real issues. They are simply waiting for their leaders to wake up and cast their ballots for those priorities as well.

Staying True to Our Values

Lieutenant Governor
Kathleen Kennedy Townsend

As Maryland's first woman lieutenant governor, KATHLEEN KENNEDY TOWNSEND *took on the issues that Marylanders cared about most, from improving schools to fighting crime, from economic development to ensuring that children and seniors get the quality health care they deserve. Prior to that, Mrs. Townsend served as deputy assistant attorney general of the United States. She has taught foreign policy at the University of Pennsylvania and the University of Maryland, Baltimore County; she serves on the board of directors of the Johns Hopkins School of Advanced International Studies; and she is a lifetime member of the Council on Foreign Relations. In 2000 Mrs. Townsend chaired the committee that drafted the Democratic Party's platform for the presidential and congressional elections.*

TODAY WE STAND AT A CRITICAL POINT IN OUR NATION'S AND OUR party's history. This is a time for both America and the Democratic Party to define themselves anew. We are the most powerful country on earth, both economically and militarily. Our values of democracy and freedom have clearly won the ideological battle with facism and communism. In so many ways, America stands triumphant. And yet we feel vulnerable and insecure. We are facing new threats. Threats that are far different from those we have ever faced before. Terrorism that no longer strikes just abroad but also at home. Weapons of mass destruction wielded by peoples who hate us simply because of who we are. These terrorists and the rogue nations that support them fear modernity, demean women, and cling to a belief system antagonistic to democracy, human rights, and economic progress. And in the age of globalization, the sea that once insulated us is now easily crossed.

The question is what are we going to do about it? As Democrats—the oldest political party in the world—we have a special responsibility to make sure that our country stays true to its values. This has been our role from the beginning and we cannot abdicate it now. We must protect ourselves from threats from abroad. At the same time we must undertake the hard work necessary to encourage freedom-loving people all around the world— and we must realize that doing so is the surest way to strengthen and protect ourselves. In the long run, the spread of freedom and democracy and democratic values will protect our national security.

For far too long, Democrats have been ceding the territory of foreign policy and national security to Republicans. Too many people have seen these as Republican issues and too many Democrats have sat back and accepted this state of affairs. But it wasn't always this way. One doesn't have to remember too far back to recall a different era. When my uncle, John Kennedy, was president, Democrats led the way on foreign policy and national security. We must recapture that ground for the good of our party and the good of the nation.

In order to make all of this happen, real changes are needed. First, we must outline a clear strategy for national defense. We must take concrete steps to stem the spread of nuclear, chemical, and biological weapons. This spring is the fortieth anniversary of the Partial Test Ban Treaty. As I write this, President Bush is taking us to war to halt Iraq from building weapons of mass destruction. But he has done little to stop other countries from following a similar course. We can no longer afford to do foreign policy like a jigsaw puzzle, putting together small pieces one at a time. We need an overarching strategy. As Democrats, we must call the president and the Republican Party to task on this failure.

Similarly, we must hold them accountable for lax homeland security. After September 11, President Bush made grand promises about homeland security. Some of them have been backed up. But to this point, there has been far too much talk about what we need to do and far too little actual doing. Ports need to be protected, water needs to be safe, cities and states need assistance. The federal government cannot leave it to the states to provide fifty versions of homeland security. The states have a critical role to play, but they simply cannot afford to make all the necessary changes on their own. We need federal dollars, planning, and leadership. We are facing a threat we have never faced before and we need to face it together as a unified nation. The federal government needs to step up to the plate and deliver the resources necessary to make this happen.

Yet at a time when we need more resources than ever, President Bush is trying to push a reckless tax cut that will cost us dearly while benefiting only the wealthiest few Americans. This could not come at a worse time. Our economy is stagnant, the government is not taking in enough revenue to pay for the programs we have, we have expensive new needs in homeland security, and the president wants to slash taxes for the wealthy. The math just doesn't add up. Democrats need to be saying this loud and clear. Make no mistake about it: this tax policy won't just make it harder to pay for homeland security, it will affect our entire economy. What Democrats need to be doing right now is reminding America of the lessons we learned about the economy during the three administrations that preceded President George W. Bush. In a nutshell, that lesson can be summed up as this: deficits are not good for the economy. That's what President Clinton realized. That's what Alan Greenspan preached to the nation. President Clinton came into office with huge deficits and left office with huge surpluses. He worked hard to eliminate deficits and balance the budget, because we had learned from the previous two Republican administrations that running up deficits only runs our economy into the ground.

We all know this. But where are the voices crying in the wilderness now? Democrats must be that voice in the wilderness. Democrats must stand up and cry out for sane fiscal policy.

We have always been known as the party that stands up for the less fortunate. FDR helped lead us out of the Depression with a whole host of trailblazing policies. Presidents Kennedy and Johnson led a war on poverty and focused our nation clearly on the ills that we face within. Democrats have always spoken for the voiceless and stood up for those who can't always stand up for themselves. Today, the Republicans are chipping apart the programs we have built, the very core of what Democrats have fought so hard for. We cannot let that happen. We need to stand up and fight against this trend. That is our proud legacy and it is something we will always be proud to do.

But Democrats have other proud legacies as well and we must not forget them now. We were once trailblazers in foreign policy, national defense, and economic policy. In order to keep America safe and put our economy back on the right track, Democrats must once again reclaim this mantle.

We can do it. But it won't be easy. We Democrats are going to need to change the way we think about our nation, our world, and ourselves. We need to break out of old bad habits, we need to remember our forebears, and we need to march forward confidently. As we do this, the party of Jefferson and Jackson, Roosevelt and Truman, Kennedy and King, will once again lead the way and America will proudly stand triumphant in battle and a beacon of hope to those fighting for freedom, justice, and equality.

Force Fields and Paradigms

Robert S. Walker

ROBERT S. WALKER *is a former member of Congress from Penn-sylvania's 16th District who now serves as chairman of Wexler & Walker Public Policy Associates, a Washington-based public-policy and consulting company. While in Congress he served in the Republican leadership as chief deputy whip, leadership chairman, and speaker pro tempore. He was chairman of the House Science Committee and vice chairman of the Budget Committee. In 2002 President Bush named him chairman of the Commission on the Future of the United States Aerospace Industry, and in 2003 the White House chose him to serve on the President's Commission on the United States Postal Service. Walker is a writer, lecturer, adviser, and commentator on technology, science, space, energy, and political issues.*

TWENTY-FIRST-CENTURY INFORMATION TECHNOLOGY HAS PROvided greater access to popular culture. The wealth of knowledge available on any imaginable topic provides every American unparalleled opportunity to focus intently on individual interests. With highly individualized attractions of popular culture more accessible and often more interesting than the issues of governance and economics, we are becoming uniquely divided.

The elections of November 2002 demonstrated some of the effects of increasing cultural division on economics and governance. We saw:

- Americans alienated from the messages of the media, university, and urban elite;
- The power of the presidency to rally the country in times of intense national focus;
- The need for big answers to the questions of modern complexity;
- And the development of cultural "force fields" that command greater public loyalty than traditional political organizations.

The loss of elite clout was evident because the country no longer relies on information controlled by these elites. Instead, Americans have turned to their own communication sources that reflect their own particular interests.

Today everyone can immerse themselves in the pursuits that

most enthuse them. They may be family related, employment related, hobby related, or even the latest television "reality" show. For instance, not too long ago television consisted of three network channels and a handful of independents. Today there are dozens of channels catering to every facet of American culture, from the food channel to the golf channel, the game show channel, the speed channel, and the science fiction channel. All news all the time on several networks has provided alternative current events coverage. The cogent factor here is the public's reliance on sources of information that are distinctly non-elite and even scorned by the elite.

Except for those citizens whose personal interests run to politics or economics, there is less affiliation with political organizations and usually less election participation. Important individual connections are now tied to organized activities centered on personal passions. We have self-organized ourselves into self-selected associations that reflect our most passionate interests—force fields.

Electrical force fields are created by energy where a charge is surrounded by a field that grows weaker as it progresses outward from the charge. The power at the center of cultural force fields is the energy of passionate belief or involvement with causes, people, programs, and things. Because the force fields are organized around individual interests, they are difficult to understand and manage in a political context.

Automobile enthusiasts can pursue their interest on thousands of websites, in hundreds of magazines, by watching television devoted to cars. They can join innumerable organizations, peruse catalogs filled with specialized merchandise, and attend any of thousands of events. They can interact with millions of people worldwide who share their passion. Any day, every day, they can spend as much time as they can spare in the world of automotive fervor. But no political agenda naturally flows from their focus.

Today's political reality is that lives filled with individual zeal supported by highly specific force fields have little time for or interest in wider pursuits. What was once a shared sense of national understanding is a distinctly different concept in a force field world.

Crisis and tragedy create an exception. Incidents such as the 9/11 attacks or the explosion of a space shuttle momentarily break through the force fields, send people to common communication outlets, and provide a sense of nationally shared experience. At the center of attention at such moments is usually the president of the United States. And that phenomenon has significant political implications.

Throughout 2002, Democrats marveled at President Bush's popularity despite bad economic news. The class warfare arguments that normally worked at such times were ineffective. The reason was that the reference point for most Americans was not so much the economy but the president and his strong leadership performance following the 9/11 attacks.

President Bush and his team seemed to have a better grasp of the changed circumstances. As his stature rose and held, he turned the national focus toward a commonly held value—security. (Democrats have long assumed that in Social Security the emphasis of most Americans is on the word *social* when in fact the term *security* is much more effective.) By pursuing the theme of economic, homeland, and national security, the president took control of the national agenda. And when he willingly expended political capital gained in the wake of 9/11, he took control of the election message and helped elect Republican candidates who shared his agenda.

The formula used by President Bush and in the mid-1990s by congressional Republicans may offer the key to political success in an era of force field focus. In the elections of both 1994 and 2002, Republicans broke through by working for paradigmatic change. GOP candidates ran on big ideas both times. In 1994 the issue was congressional reform and balanced budgets. In 2002 the political landscape was defined by homeland and national security issues.

Consider the nature of some of the more intractable problems faced by our nation today and how a change of paradigm could be appealing.

Government has become increasingly dysfunctional. Decisions take so long that they constantly fall behind the rapidity of technological change. Agencies that should cooperate on common missions compete instead. Decisions are made inside vertical, programmatic "silos" when horizontal management across programs and agencies is needed. The Department of Homeland Security was necessary because of the lack of agency cooperation in an arena that suddenly became critical.

But restructuring government should not await crisis. Paradigmatic change should involve Congress revising committee jurisdictions and structures. Departments and agencies should create paths for broad use of resources rather than jealously guarding narrow objectives. Continued use of individual budget streams for individual agencies funded by narrowly focused congressional committees is a recipe for ongoing government dysfunction and a model for failure in a fast-paced global economy.

Education has failed to acknowledge the societal shift toward individualism. Instead the bulk of public education curricula remain designed to prepare students for work in an increasingly downsized industrial economy.

Paradigmatic change in education would require the adoption of individualized instructional programs where student interests and talents are at the center of learning. Teachers' roles would change, as they become information managers in the classroom rather than imparters of information.

Access to limitless energy resources and the need for environmental integrity are rivals inside today's political framework. Proposals to increase energy production are consistently met with environmental opposition, and zero emission environmental proposals are seen as threatening to energy security.

Paradigmatic change would anticipate an unlimited supply of energy for industrial, residential, business, and transportation use without the penalty of environmental degradation. The creation of a hydrogen economy holds that promise.

Health care has become centralized, bureaucratic, and incapable of delivering quality at affordable prices. Paradigmatic change would offer broad individual health care choice, responsiveness to technological and pharmaceutical advances, and economic availability in every community.

Congressional Republicans recognized the power of such big ideas in the Contract with America back in 1994. The contract proposed major institutional reforms inside the U.S. House of

Representatives. That big idea helped swell voter ranks in an off-year election and a massive GOP victory resulted.

Under the direction of Speaker Newt Gingrich, Congress also drove paradigmatic economic change in the earliest days of the Republican revolution. House Republicans defied elite analysis and conventional wisdom by shutting down the operation of much of the federal government to force action on a balanced budget. Instant analysis predicted that this politically unpopular and risky move would cost the Republicans the next congressional election. Instead, they won the national debate. President Clinton was forced to propose a balanced budget, the political dialogue changed from tax increases and deficits to tax cuts and balanced budgets, and the Republicans ultimately retained their House majority.

The untold story of the present Bush administration initiatives is the willingness to address issues large enough to penetrate force fields. Social Security and Medicare reform, energy security through a switch to hydrogen, restructuring and transformation of governmental functions, and education reform directed toward the learning of every child are well beyond the incremental steps usually proposed by incumbent administrations.

Improved information technology has created a new challenge for national leaders. With the American people immersed in individualized pursuit of popular culture, political loyalty and affiliation have become increasingly irrelevant to their lives. The leadership challenge is to have the courage to advance bold ideas that go beyond poll-tested fluff. Bold ideas will assure the continued desirability of democratic participation in the force field environment where Americans now insulate themselves.

A Vision for the Future

Congressman J. C. Watts, Jr.

After eight years in the United States Congress, four of which he spent as part of the Republican leadership, J. C. WATTS, JR., is now the founder and chairman of the J.C. Watts Companies, a consulting and public affairs group. Congressman Watts is also giving speeches, writing, and serving as chairman of GOPAC. He currently resides with his family in Oklahoma.

ON SEPTEMBER 11, 2001, AFTER A YEAR OF VICIOUS PARTISAN feuding, the leadership of Congress found themselves evacuated to a secret bunker. There we sat, not as Democrats and Republicans but as Americans. I hadn't seen many nonpartisan moments in my years in Congress. This was something extraordinary. The partisan politics that had followed the presidential election disappeared in the smoke and rubble of September 11. But more than that, I believe our country underwent a fundamental shift as images and emotions of that day were forever seared on our national psyche.

Today, America sees our role in the world differently. We see our responsibility for the lives of others in need through a new prism of pride and pain. And we understand far better what is really important in this world: family, faith, community, and country. In the months, and now years, that have followed, the American people have made something clear. With the country at war, they want no return to the bitter partisan politics that have always seemed to characterize Washington. And for a time, I do think both sides did their best to avoid partisan rancor.

But the bipartisan spirit always seems to end. During the 2002 elections partisan politics reemerged as an ever-present and powerful force. To Democrats the president and his allies could do nothing right. To Republicans he had done nothing wrong. However, the successes of the education bill, the faith-based initiative, tax cuts, and the war on terrorism were the coattails that Republicans rode to historic midterm election victories.

But partisanship was back in Washington. This is not a surprise, but rather a continuation of a cycle that moves from bipartisan unity in times of national crisis to partisan bickering when the crisis ends or can be ignored. This cycle is fueled by history, tradition, and the ideology of the left and the right. These issues have been with us for a long time, and it will take a new perspective and new ideas to move our nation forward to win the war on terror, to improve the economy, and to secure America's future.

On the left, many still see problems from a more emotional point of view. They believe that their ideas and proposals are morally superior and that they are anointed protectors of the common people against the hordes of elitist conservative infidels. In their world, all government spending is good; all tax cuts are bad and the only source of federal deficits. They never met a government program they didn't like, and help for disadvantaged Americans doesn't count unless it comes from the government. Hollywood is never held accountable for creating the increasingly valueless culture in which our children grow up. Their philosophy says if it feels good, do it. If you don't want to, don't. If it's a nuisance, abort it. If you don't like it, divorce it.

But that's only half the Washington problem. On the right, many see their mission as divinely inspired and themselves as saviors of America's traditional values from the evil forces of liberalism. In their world, all government social programs are bad. Compassion is weakness. Personal responsibility is the panacea for every problem. Their philosophy represents a black-and-white world in which there is only right or wrong—no shades of gray. Compromise is anathema, and strict adherence to conservative dogma is demanded.

In spite of what I think, or what the far left or far right thinks, we are not a right-wing or left-wing country. The American people exist somewhere in the middle, probably slightly right of center. They reject what they perceive as the often insensitive moralizing of conservatives just as they refuse to accept what they see as the moral relativism of extreme liberals. Yet the far right and the far left dominate news coverage and drive the political debate in Washington. I believe people are looking for something more from their elected leaders, something different.

They want solutions. They want a civil tone in Washington, less fighting and more progress. The American people have moved beyond their political leaders, and we need to catch up. We need to stop fighting yesterday's battles and quit blaming the other side for past wrongs and behavior, real or imagined, to justify our own actions. We need less stereotyping, fewer ideological confrontations, and the wisdom to understand that when a nation is as politically divided as this one has been in recent years, there are times when working with one another and building coalitions may be the only way to achieve progress.

Members of Congress in both parties have some changing to do to meet the new expectations of the American people and make this country all it can be. That doesn't mean Republicans or Democrats can't point out the difference between our parties' approaches to solving problems and argue forcefully for our causes. That was part of my job description as a member of the Republican leadership; more to the point, it's what democracy is all about.

I am convinced that the principles of the Republican Party offer the best prescription for what ails us as a country. So, a strong, viable Republican Party is important to me as a conservative but also as a parent, an American of African descent, and a Christian. But if Republicans want to grow the party for a better tomorrow, we need to ask ourselves some tough questions today.

Is the Republican Party listening hard enough to what

America is saying? Do we really hear when people talk or are we just paying lip service with the expected response? Can we remain true to the traditions and fundamental principles upon which this party is based—freedom, opportunity, the rights and responsibilities of the individual, and smaller government—and still be open-minded to differing points of view? Is it enough to be right? Are we reaching out to people of every color, religion, ethnicity, and region to invite them to join our cause?

When it comes to our future, I don't think the Democratic Party can get this country where it needs to go. I believe deeply that the values and ideas of the Republican Party will do far more to help people find the promised land if we are willing to lead.

But the world is changing quickly and in so many directions. If we are going to be the majority party of the future, we must not remain chained to the past. So after much soul-searching, I have come to the conclusion that the moment has come for a new conservative vision—one that preserves the basic values of our party but throws open the door to new ideas and new people. We must adopt a "New Conservative Strategy for a Better America," a three-part vision for the future.

First, we must renew our commitment to the nation's fundamental values and rebuild our core strength: the family. Second, each of us must do our part to make compassion and diversity central to American life. We have to reach out to conservative and moderate blacks, Hispanics, and other Democrats and independents willing to join George W. Bush, J. C. Watts, and other Republicans with whom they share both goals and values. And finally, we must enthusiastically embrace new models and ideas to meet the challenges ahead. We can't govern in the twenty-first century the way we did in the 1970s, '80s, and '90s by simply defining the left. We must offer an alternative—a conservative vision of opportunity, quality education, and economic and retirement security for every American.

Through this vision, I am convinced that we can make this a better place for every American: a better place to raise our children, to provide opportunity here at home, and to advance the cause of humanity and freedom around the world.

Jim Crow, Republican Style: Voter Suppression in 2002

Professor Sean Wilentz

SEAN WILENTZ *is Dayton-Stockton Professor of History and director of the Program in American Studies at Princeton University. He is the author of numerous books and essays on American history and politics, and is currently completing a book on the rise of American democracy from Jefferson to Lincoln.*

THE GREATEST SCANDAL OF THE 2002 ELECTIONS WAS THE REPUBlican attempt to suppress the voting rights of minorities. Across the nation, and especially in the South, Republican operatives engaged in partisan efforts to confound and intimidate black and other minority voters. The Republicans, led by Republican National Committee chairman Marc Racicot, also raised trumped-up charges that Democrats were guilty of voter fraud. Every one of the Republicans' charges has been fully refuted. Every case of Republican voter suppression has been fully documented.

The Republicans' campaign was of a piece with their earlier successful efforts to strip minority voters of their basic civil rights. The dubious outcome of the 2000 presidential campaign, for example, hinged on many things—and one of the most important was the purging, or so-called scrubbing, of thousands of eligible black Florida voters from the polling lists by Republican state authorities, under the aegis of Secretary of State Katherine Harris.

Two years later, Republicans brazenly redeployed those winning tactics. Not since the era of Jim Crow, when racist southern Democrats were the suppressors, has the nation seen reports of such large-scale blatant partisan attacks on minority voting rights. And there is strong reason to believe, especially given the indifference displayed by most political reporters and commentators in 2002, that in the future the Republicans will expand their attacks, under the direct supervision of the party's highest leadership in Washington.

In Florida, where in 2000 a howling mob composed chiefly of Republican congressional aides shut down the counting of votes, a combination of high-tech and low-tech suppression tactics came into play in 2002. In Miami-Dade County, site of the 2000 mob violence, a shadowy GOP group backing Governor Jeb Bush tried to pack the polling places with hundreds of its own intimidating overseers. The effort was explicitly racial, as exposed in a financial appeal on the group's behalf by the ultra-right-wing pro-Republican website NewsMax.com, urging a massive counterattack on Florida's black voters. At the very last minute, a local judge blocked the poll-packing scheme. But no court could head off the vicious Republican telemarketing scheme (one of many that the Republicans mounted around the nation in 2002) that instructed Florida's disproportionately black Democratic voters to cast their absentee ballots after Election Day—at which point they would no longer be counted.

Maryland Republicans targeted minority voters more crudely. In Baltimore, anonymous flyers appeared in predominantly black neighborhoods, giving the wrong election date and containing language that strongly—and falsely—implied that they would be barred from voting if they had any outstanding parking tickets, if their rent was overdue, or if they had any outstanding warrants. Prior to the election, a spokesman for the Republicans' Maryland gubernatorial candidate, Bob Ehrlich, let slip to a reporter that their campaign tactics would include deploying off-duty uniformed policemen as poll watchers.

In Arkansas, paid campaign workers for incumbent Republican senator Tim Hutchinson showed up at one polling place, harassed election officials and black voters (taking the photographs of those who would not be turned away), and disrupted balloting until they were finally forcibly removed from the premises. During Louisiana's senatorial runoff in December, Republican officials bribed black youths with $75 apiece to hold aloft ready-made, crudely designed signs in black neighborhoods saying: "Mary: If you don't respect us, don't expect us"—an effort to play race card politics against Democratic Senate incumbent Mary Landrieu. (This was one of the very few incidents reported fleetingly in the national press. *The New York Times* reported straightforwardly that "the Republicans did their best to suppress the black vote so crucial to Ms. Landrieu's fortunes." But the report came and went.)

In Texas, two Republican poll monitors in separate towns became so abusive in their harassment of elderly Hispanic voters that they had to be taken away by the police. The Hidalgo County, Texas, elections commissioner banned one Republican operative named Tom Haughey from appearing at all early polling stations in order to prevent him from disrupting the work of presiding judges and election clerks.

Republican racial targeting was not confined to the Deep South. In Michigan, for example, the Republican state committee mobilized hundreds of poll monitors whose mission was clearly to challenge minority voters and so dampen minority turnout in Detroit and a few other cities. And in other states, including New Hampshire, New Jersey, and Indiana, Republican multi-dialing phone operations, possibly located out of state, either harassed Democratic voters, regardless of race, with annoying repeated calls purportedly from Democratic candidates or jammed Democratic lines on Election Day in order to smother Democratic get-out-the-vote efforts.

How much of this was coordinated, and how much of it by the upper echelons of the Republican Party, is difficult to say without a comprehensive and impartial investigation. But there are grounds for believing that the suppression efforts involved more than isolated dirty tricks or a few overzealous poll watchers.

In 2000, Republican House whip (now majority leader) Tom

DeLay was an instigator of the postelection effort to prevent the votes from being counted in Florida. His aides helped lead the so-called bourgeois riot that stopped the recount in Miami-Dade County. In the 2002 elections, DeLay organized something he called STOMP, the Strategic Taskforce to Organize and Mobilize People. DeLay and his minions' involvement in voter suppression efforts in districts across the country went uninvestigated.

The example of the Republican Leadership Council and its executive director, Allen Raymond, is also instructive. The RLC is a partisan Republican campaign group that includes eight U.S. senators on its advisory board. In 2002, Raymond was its executive director. Raymond also runs a telemarketing firm called GOP Marketplace—a firm now under investigation by federal and state authorities for sabotaging Democratic phone-banks in New Hampshire and, perhaps, in other states. And, as it happens, the RLC, according to a filing with the Internal Revenue Service, paid GOP Marketplace nearly $30,000 on November 4, 2002— the day before the election—for "phone bank" operations. Not only does it look as if Raymond was paying himself with Republican money, it also looks as if GOP Marketplace may have been doing its dirty work on behalf of the RLC—and not just in New Hampshire.

Then there is the case of Marc Racicot and the RNC. In an effort to deflect the growing reports of Republican intimidation, Chairman Racicot loudly trumpeted countercharges about a handful of voter fraud incidents allegedly undertaken by Democratic officials. The loudest of these involved what the RNC called wholesale fraudulent registration of Indians in South Dakota, where incumbent Democrat Tim Johnson was involved in a tight

URGENT NOTICE

COME OUT TO VOTE ON NOVEMBER 6TH

BEFORE YOU COME TO VOTE MAKE SURE YOU PAY YOUR

- ## PARKING TICKETS
- ## MOTOR VEHICLE TICKETS
- ## OVERDUE RENT

AND MOST IMPORTANT ANY WARRANTS

Anonymous flyer posted in Baltimore, Maryland, black neighborhoods, Election Day, November 5, 2002

reelection race. By the time the Republican smoke had cleared, however, it turned out that the fraud amounted to no more than the accidental enrollment of a tiny number of voters by a single contracted election worker. Other RNC charges, involving alleged Democratic fraud in Arkansas and elsewhere, proved equally baseless. Yet the RNC succeeded in muddying the waters, turning the real story of Republican voter suppression into a false "both-sides-do-it" story—with conservative Fox News taking the lead.

How effective were the Republicans' suppression efforts in 2002? Given that statewide Democratic candidates in Arkansas and Louisiana won anyway, while Democrats in New Hampshire, Florida, and Texas lost, the record seems, at best, mixed. But that is no reason to be lulled into assuming they will not be more energized and successful in the future, especially when the 2004 Republican campaign is expected to be the best-financed in history. How much of this will involve Republican suppression of the Democratic vote, and especially of minority voters? The evidence from 2002—and from 2000 in Florida—are clear portents.

The 2002 Elections

John Zogby

President and CEO of Zogby International, an independent polling firm, JOHN ZOGBY polls politics regularly for Reuters, NBC News, and major daily newspapers nationwide.

IN THE CLOSING WEEKS OF THE 2002 ELECTIONS, DEMOCRATS complained that they were unable to get their message out to voters because they were effectively blocked by a popular president who was engaged in saber-rattling against Iraq, beating the drums of war. Because of President George W. Bush's high personal favorable ratings after the September 11 terrorist attacks, Democrats were wary of attacking such a popular figure. And because they feared being tarnished as unpatriotic and weak on defense, many leading Senate and House Democrats fell in line behind the president in support for war in Iraq and even endorsed a preemptive strike.

Much of the above is true, with one glaring exception: it is hard to discern any Democratic message in 2002 at all. The top two issues in the election were war and the economy. In the former, the Democrats posed no alternative to voters. Voters never select a "me too" party if they can get the real thing. On the economy, the best they could come up with was a middle-class tax cut as opposed to Bush's plan, which favored the rich. This despite the fact that populist "us vs. them" rhetoric has not worked for the Democrats for decades. And tax cuts have never been popular with voters in general or with core Democratic and key swing voters.

In the past decade voters have internalized the Republican message about government: they fear deficits and they do not trust grand promises. While Democrats could have scored points with small reforms in health care and education, they seemed to lose their will.

In short, in an election when the prominent national mood was one of insecurity and anxiety, Democrats had nothing new to say and no compelling persona to say it.

Now, not everything can be blamed on the Democrats. With 66 percent of likely voters saying before the election that they owned 401(k) or other stock investments, no action by either party could have relieved this group's anger or fear of the future. Indeed, this group—which looked like it might vote anti-incumbent—actually ended up voting Republican.

And no one could have guessed that President Bush would risk his popularity by vigorously campaigning in fifteen states with tight Senate and House races in the last days of the campaign. In a period of high anxiety, voters were looking for some kind of— any kind of—leadership. President Bush offered it in a vacuum by being present.

An issue that worked in the favor of the Republicans in 2002 was abortion. While a majority of Americans are still pro-choice, the issue of late-term abortions actually has both caused a shift of about ten to twelve points away from pro-choice (67–69 percent a few years ago to 57 percent now) and increased intensity among pro-life voters. We found this in our postelection polling in many states with close races.

While the Republicans made history in an off-election year by gaining seats, the United States is still a fifty-fifty nation. Even with the president's popularity at the time of the 2002 election, he improved the Republican share of the vote by only 1 percent— from 48 percent to 49 percent. Thus there are real opportunities for the Democrats. First, the president has not built, nor curiously has he sought to build, a governing majority. From the outset of his administration, he has defined his presidency as a right-wing one on key issues like energy, the environment, and abortion. He has made little effort to attract swing voters as he did when he was governor of Texas.

Second, he has squandered the goodwill he achieved after the events of September 11. A close look at his polling numbers as of this writing reveals that he has solid support among Republicans, whites, men, conservatives, rural voters, married couples, and investors. Independents are split and Democrats are hostile.

His numbers are back to just about where they were when he became president in January 2001 and just before September 11—about fifty-fifty.

And his adventurous foreign policy has the nation split as we prepare for a war against Iraq. His administration has severely damaged the United Nations Security Council, NATO, and the image of the United States in the rest of the world.

At the same time, the Democrats face some grave challenges. There is a serious values deficit. In addition to losing out to Republicans on family values, the Democrats score low among voters—including key swing groups—on the issue of integrity.

Democrats are salivating about the appearance of a book in 2002 called *The Emerging Democratic Majority,* which foretells the growth of key Democratic-leaning demographics in the next decade. But I think more important than demographics in understanding voting behavior is how voters identify themselves. Thus, the real growth over the next few years will be among self-identified investors—a group that has been voting more Republican than Democrat.

The Democrats are going to have to satisfy their liberal core base and swing voters at the same time. One issue that can help them is the war against Iraq. A principled stand in opposition to this kind of foreign policy can satisfy the many Americans who have serious issues with the Bush administration. One important lesson for Democrats: every Democrat who opposed the congressional resolution endorsing a first strike against Iraq was reelected in 2002.

Here is an outline of the sorts of things that I think will aid the Democrats in building a winning coalition:

1. *Prescription Drugs*. Despite the fact that the era of big government is over, voters consistently prefer an expansion of Medicare coverage to include prescription drugs. This includes strong support from fifty- to sixty-nine-year-olds who are normally this country's most reliable conservatives. They are the sandwich generation who are paying for college costs and elderly parents. Democrats could pick off some of this solid Republican group. Demographics are not always destiny.

2. *Social Security*. Why can't Americans have both a lockbox to protect older Americans (both those on Social Security and those close to retirement) and some form of modest personal savings alternative for younger voters (the most libertarian of voters who distrust government)? Stealing this issue could be a real coup for Democrats.

3. *Foreign Policy*. The legacy of the Bush administration might very well be the mess caused by our relations with almost every nation on the planet. Democrats will do well by working to restore our image in the world. A good start would be to endorse the Kyoto Treaty, the World Criminal Court, and the United Nations effort on the HIV-AIDS pandemic. This must be within the context of a broader vision that seeks to achieve better multilateral relations and decision-making.

4. *Tax Cuts*. Very few Americans want to go back to huge deficits. And Americans are willing to pay higher taxes if they are getting something in return.

5. *Tolerance*. The one "traditional value" that Democrats score best on in my polling is tolerance. This country has

an unfortunate legacy of intolerance in times of war—but no one ever looks at those periods with fond memories. Democrats have an important issue here with the Bush administration: Does national security mean having to lose that which actually defines us as a people and a nation?

One step in this direction may be to define a bigger tent that includes pro-life Democrats. Democrats cannot afford litmus tests if they want to be a majority party.

Another step in opening up the big tent and building a majority is for Democrats to welcome new groups like Muslims and South Asians, two rapidly growing groups.

Finally, Democrats need new ideas. One way to develop them is to take a page from conservative leader Grover Norquist's book of success. Norquist of the Americans for Tax Reform hosts a weekly forum every Wednesday and welcomes a diversity of opinions in a free-for-all discussion format. Perhaps the Democrats could be more open to new ideas and less dependent on prescribed limits on their thinking by their interest subgroups.

Acknowledgments

WHILE I WAS WORKING ON THIS BOOK I WAS CONSTANTLY AMAZED by the rate of change in the world. Post 9/11, international and domestic affairs seemed to change in a matter of days—often radically. In today's world, effective politics and government are even more essential.

American politics at its best is an open, energized debate over competing visions and ideas. Our founding fathers were people of deeply held convictions and opinions, and they pursued them with passion and strength. Jefferson, Adams, Madison, and Hamilton framed our political system not as a harmonious choir but as an arena of fierce debate and ultimately intelligent compromise. I applaud those who enter the arena, as Teddy Roosevelt said, whether by seeking elected office, working in government, volunteering at a not-for-profit, or debating political issues around the dining room table. This book seeks to encourage and inform that debate.

This volume was made possible through the tireless efforts of many people. Most important, I would like to thank the outstanding contributors who reflected upon this critical period in American politics and provided provocative essays in a short period of time.

I want to thank Will Murphy and Random House and Jim Griffin of the William Morris Agency for making this book a reality. Special thanks to Jim Kessler, who did much of the editing, and Jeremy Creelan and Jon Cowan, who crafted and debated the policy ideas in this book as well as in my campaign and at HUD. Sincere gratitude to Rhoda Glickman, my dear friend, colleague, and confidant in all my endeavors, for bringing together many of the contributors. Thanks to Jill Brooke for her journalistic advice and help. Many thanks to my Random House team: Kate Blum, Brian McLendon, Evelyn O'Hara, and Janet Wygal. And thanks to Ashley Cotton for putting together the entire project.

As a visiting fellow at Harvard, I had an outstanding class at the Institute of Politics at the Kennedy School of Government, who acted as the editorial committee to review these essays. They are an impressive group of young people, and I believe I learned more than I taught. I thank former Secretary of Agriculture Dan Glickman, the head of the Institute of Politics and my close friend and colleague, for his help. Many thanks to Harvard president

Larry Summers, former secretary of the treasury, for his guidance and friendship.

Last year I ran for governor of New York, and while the campaign was not ultimately successful, I am proud of the effort's contribution to the public dialogue. We raised issues that needed attention and put forth real solutions to problems long neglected. We also made a political campaign what it should be—fun. And we developed lifelong friendships and strong bonds in the process. A most sincere thank you to my extended family: Cheryl and Blair Effron, Carolyn and Laurence Belfer, Fred Hochberg and Tom Healy, Leslie Stern, Ira Riklis, Liz and Kent Swig, Kimora Lee and Russell Simmons, Ethel Kennedy, Senator Ted Kennedy, Joe, Patrick, and the entire Kennedy family, Abbie, Neil, and the entire Cole family, Cristina Greevan Cuomo, Rainer Greevan, and the entire Greevan family, Beth and Ron Dozoretz, Aby Rosen, Michael and Kris Fuchs, Tonja and Ed Davidson, Joyce and Vincent Tese, Cathy and Efi Gildor, Mayor Jerry Jennings, Bobby Shriver, Nazee and Joseph Moinian, Audrey and Marvin Schein, Donna Marino, David Emil, Debbie Hymowitz, Geraldine Ferraro, Jerry Colonna, Loretta and Steven Dym, Joy McManigal and Giancarlo Esposito, Sandy and Floss Frucher, Trey and Doug Teitelbaum, Dini Von Mueffling and Matt Gohd, Nancy Hollander and Ken Sunshine, Tondra and Jeffrey Lynford, Christina Perpignano, Tom Downey, Harriet and George McDonald, Tom Mulroy, Mary Porcelli, Nancy and Bill O'Shaughnessy, my running mate in the governor's race, Charlie King, Royce Mulholland, Lucille Falcone and Doug Menagh, Mona Ackerman, Brad Scheler, Marvin Rosen, Ted, Marie, and the Vecchio family, Nancy, Bob, and the Mazzola family, John Dyson, Tonio Burgos, Phil Piccigallo, John Belizaire, Doug Harmon, Paul Francis, Dino Lombardi, Jay Snyder, Amy and Jim Chanos, Joseph Bigica, Betsy Cohn, Valerie and Michael Rozen, Robert Zimmerman, Jan Atlas, Jimmy Iovine, Domna Stanton, Betty Cotton, Jill Iscol, Mark Weingarten, Scott Elkins and Charles Myers, Lynda Carter, Robert Altman, John Coale, Barry Appelman, Paul Zevnick, Ginny Grenham, Claire and Al Dwoskin, Paul Polo, Allison and Barry Berke, Corrie and Jon Sandelman, Sarah and Peter Beshar, Scott Resnick, Dan Berger, Dan Stern, Scott Delman, Orin Snyder, Peter Parcher, Morty Bahr, Steven Hayes, Christopher Barley and Jonathan Sheffer, Gary Goldstein, John Catsimatidis, Sandi Farkas, Jim Runsdorf, Richie Ebers, John Sweeney, Dena and Andy McKelvey, Andrew Murstein, Michael King, Ted Fields, Lucy and Richard Halperin, Adam Clayton Powell IV, Lisa and Richard Baker, Daniel Ziff, Billy Baldwin, Joey Pantoliano, Lawrence Mancino, Martin Luther King III, Scott Rechler, Stacy and Jonathan Levine, John Halpern, Peter Hochfelder, David Simon, Ann and Andrew Tisch, Christie Brinkley and Peter Cooke, Rick Ostroff, Nancy Jacobson and Mark Penn, Jim Keppler, Dana Kirkpatrick, Gary Foster, Sant Chatwal, Robin Bronk, the H.E.L.P. USA Team, and my entire finance committee.

Thanks to my "other brothers": campaign treasurer Richard Sirota, advisor Dan Klores, mentor Mike Del Giudice, counselor John Marino, buddy Jeffrey Sachs, businessman extraordinaire Andrew Farkas, and financial whiz Gregg Hymowitz; and my brothers-in-law and in-spirit, Kenneth Cole, Brian O'Donohue, and Howard Maier.

Thanks to my great campaign team: Joe Percoco, my loyal and brave friend and right hand through the effort; Bridget Siegel, whose undefeatable and indefatigable spirit led an amazingly successful fund-raising team; Peter Ragone, who dealt with the New York press corps and made it look easy; Josh Isay, who spearheaded the entire effort; Alex Stanton, who was a great deputy campaign manager. I was fortunate to have outstanding and dedicated colleagues and volunteers on the campaign trail whom I will never forget, and the only order in which they can be placed is alphabetical: Beverly Alston, Ari Bassin, Mary Pat Bonner, Michael Borden, Megan Brewster, Stu Brody, Kelly Calanni, Andrew Cantor, Dennis Cheng, Jeremy Creelan, Jill Daschle, Bill de Blasio, Jacques De Graff, Amy Dolan, Jennifer Eason Hanley, Brian Ebert, Gabrielle Fialkoff, Adam Fryer, Anselm Fusco, Raymond R. Gilliar, Howard Glaser, Juliana Goldman, Samantha Goldman, Pat Halpin, Kristin Hoppmann, Wendy Hymowitz, Mary Liz Kane, Jamie Kantrowitz, Kim Kauffman, Shane Kavanugh, Daniel Kohns, Mayur Lakhani, Micah Lasher, JC Leeler, Melvin Lowe, Brian Mahanna, Bonnie Marx, Kathleen McGlynn, Kate McKay, Cheryl Meredith, Alex Navarro, Olivier Sultan, Kirsten Powers, David Pristin, Eric Pugatch, Joe Rabito, Veena Raj, Tricia Riffenburgh, David Rosen, Jennifer Scott, Menashe Shapiro, Lenny Speiller, Kimball Stroud, Stacey Stump, Kerry Townsend Jacob, Matt Traub, Brad Tucker, Brian Turetsky, Josh Weiner, Steven Weiss, Jonathan Zalisky.

I met many outstanding Democrats around New York State during my campaign. From Oneida to Richmond counties, there are dedicated citizens working every day to secure a bright future for the children of New York. Thanks to the county chairs, state committee members, state senators, assembly members, mayors, and other officials who helped me in my goal to become New York's governor. I cherish the time, advice, and support you shared with me every day.

I most enjoy government service and the ability to make a real difference in people's lives. My eight years at HUD were both an education and a tremendous opportunity to make positive change in our country. At HUD we dealt with some of the greatest governmental challenges our nation faces: poverty, racism, income inequality, urban decay, government waste, environmental degradation, and homelessness. While we did not change the world, we did take a step forward. My greatest contribution at HUD was to assemble the best team of dedicated and talented professionals to ever lead the effort. I want to thank Jon Cowan and Jacquie Lawing, my dynamic chiefs of staff, who led the team; my deputy and friend, Saul Ramirez, my assistant secretaries Bill Apgar, Cardell Cooper, Hal DeCell, Harold Lucas, Susan Wachter, Fred Karnas, and Eva Plaza, who developed cutting-edge policy and made programs actually work; my legal counsels who kept us out of trouble while we were pushing the envelope: General Counsel Gail Laster, Nancy Lesser, Kirsten Gillibrand, Doug Kantor, Max Stier, and Kevin Simpson; my public relations guru Karen Hinton, the New York Team and great friends Bill de Blasio, Charlie King, and Allison Lee, who made New York a better state; my three friends who have been with me since our first campaign twenty years ago, who have become great attorneys and public servants and dropped what they were doing to join me at HUD: Howard Glaser, Mark Gordon, and Gary Eisenman; my head of security with whom I visited every state in the nation and countries around the world and always kept me safe and smiling, Deputy U.S. Marshall Clarence Day; our spiritual leader Father Joe Hacala; my strategist and friend Chris Lehane; the great program and operations team that made things happen: Alvin Brown, Ted Carr, Matt Franklin, Wendy Greuel, Todd Howe, Alicia Kolar, Lisa MacSpadden, Frank McNally, Lisa Patlis, Joe Percoco, Scott Sherman, Alexandra Stanton, Deborah Vincent, and Eden Williams; and my personal assistant for all eight years, who helped me run HUD and my life, Dorothea "Rita" Yorkshire.

We were part of a great federal team. I owe a tremendous debt of gratitude to President Bill Clinton for giving me the opportunity to serve as one of the youngest Cabinet secretaries in history and for his friendship over this past decade. Vice President Al Gore, the man who should be president, is a good friend and mentor to me. Henry Cisneros, HUD secretary in the first term, under whom I was honored to serve as assistant secretary. My colleagues in the administration: secretary now governor Bill Richardson, Administrator Carol Browner, Secretary Bruce Babbitt, Secretary Dan Glickman, Gene Sperling, Maggie Williams, John Podesta, Steve Ricchetti, Secretary Mickey Kantor, Secretary Rodney Slater, Jack Quinn, Ambassador Mack McLarty, Secretary Alexis Herman, Cheryl Mills, and Sandy Berger.

All lessons start at home. For me, the importance of community, politics, and government was learned at an early age. Being raised in New York City, with its density, demographics, and complexity, one instinctively learned the interconnection of different people and places, the diversity of ideas, and the need for fair and inclusive decision-making. My grandparents were the first to speak to me of the American ideal and the immigrant experience. Their life lesson was a political science course. Indeed, there were few issues that I discussed at the president's Cabinet table that I hadn't first heard at my grandparents' kitchen table.

My family has carried forth these traditions. My mother, Matilda, was a great first lady of the state of New York. Trained as a schoolteacher, she now runs an international mentoring program. My sister Maria is a super mom and wife and runs H.E.L.P.—an organization I started but that she has made the largest private provider for the homeless in the nation. My sister Margaret is a doctor, Madeline is a lawyer, and both have always been involved in community service. My brother, Christopher, is a journalist committed to the role of the Fourth Estate in keeping the system balanced. They have all supported me personally and professionally in every possible way. Kerry Kennedy Cuomo does extraordinary work on international human rights and spent years dedicated to my political efforts. I sincerely thank her.

But most of all, I thank my father, Governor Mario Cuomo, for his patience, time, teaching, and example. Like the prodigal son, I had to travel the nation and the world to realize the best model of public service was my own father. He has been a great role model, teacher, and friend, and has always been there for me. None of what I have accomplished would have been possible without him.

Credits

About the Type

This book was set in Sabon, a typeface designed by the well-known German typographer Jan Tschichold (1902–74). Sabon's design is based upon the original letter forms of Claude Garamond and was created specifically to be used for three sources: foundry type for hand composition, Linotype, and Monotype. Tschichold named his typeface for the famous Frankfurt typefounder Jacques Sabon, who died in 1580.

ANDREW CUOMO is a New York native. An attorney, at twenty-eight he founded Housing Enterprise for Less Privileged (HELP), which became the nation's largest private provider of transitional housing for the homeless. He practiced law as an assistant district attorney in Manhattan and served as campaign manager for his father, Mario M. Cuomo, in his successful 1982 race for governor of New York. At thirty-nine Andrew Cuomo was named Secretary of Housing and Urban Development in the Clinton administration and won awards from Harvard for his innovation and success at passing major legislation.

Join our nonfiction newsletter by sending a blank e-mail to:
sub_rht-nonfiction@info.randomhouse.com
or visit www.atrandom.com